GREAT LIVES OBSERVED

Gerald Emanuel Stearn, *General Editor*

EACH VOLUME IN THE SERIES VIEWS THE CHARACTER AND ACHIEVEMENT OF A GREAT WORLD FIGURE IN THREE PERSPECTIVES—THROUGH HIS OWN WORDS, THROUGH THE OPINIONS OF HIS CONTEMPORARIES, AND THROUGH RETROSPECTIVE JUDGMENTS—THUS COMBINING THE INTIMACY OF AUTOBIOGRAPHY, THE IMMEDIACY OF EYEWITNESS OBSERVATION, AND THE OBJECTIVITY OF MODERN SCHOLARSHIP.

IRVING H. SMITH, *editor of this volume in the Great Lives Observed series, is Professor of History at Sir George Williams University in Quebec, Canada. He has also served as associate editor of* Canadian Slavic Studies *for the past five years.*

GREAT LIVES OBSERVED

TROTSKY

Edited by IRVING H. SMITH

"*I have never lost my faith in the revolutionary power
of the masses. But we must be prepared for a long fight.
For years, maybe decades, of revolts, civil wars, new revolts,
new wars. And if sometimes it looks as if the class war is
flagging, the leaders crumbling under the threats and
lies of the bourgeois regime, there are always new
generations to come.*"

—PETER WEISS, Trotzki im Exil

PRENTICE-HALL, INC., ENGLEWOOD CLIFFS, N.J.

Library of Congress Cataloging in Publication Data

SMITH, IRVING H   comp.
  Trotsky.

  (Great lives observed)   (A Spectrum Book)
  Includes bibliographical references.
  I. Trotskiĭ, Lev, 1879–1940.   I. Title.
DK254.T6S54   1973   947.084′092′4 [B]   73–3226
ISBN 0–13–930974–8
ISBN 0–13–930966–7 (pbk)

PRENTICE-HALL INTERNATIONAL, INC. (*London*)
PRENTICE-HALL OF AUSTRALIA PTY., LTD. (*Sydney*)
PRENTICE-HALL OF CANADA, LTD. (*Toronto*)
PRENTICE-HALL OF INDIA PRIVATE LIMITED (*New Delhi*)
PRENTICE-HALL OF JAPAN, INC. (*Tokyo*)

Contents

v

PART TWO

THE WORLD LOOKS AT TROTSKY

For Lawrence

Introduction

With the passage of time historical figures either shrink or grow in stature. In the case of Leon Trotsky time, after a brief eclipse, has increased his image so that he appears today, for good or evil, as one of the giants of the first half of the twentieth century. The renewed interest in Trotsky's life is reflected by the numerous studies which are beginning to appear, and by the sudden availability of almost all his writings. For many of the New Left generation he has reclaimed both the prestige and the mantle of *the* revolutionary leader.

The argument supporting Trotsky's claim to importance rests on his contribution to political theory, his literary legacy, and above all his role as man of action. In Part One of this volume we have an opportunity to appraise the quality of Trotsky's thought and literary style. His analysis of social forces in Imperial Russia and his development of the idea of "permanent revolution" suggest that as a Marxist thinker he could, on the power of his own creativity, go beyond the formulations of Marx and Engels. In that sense his theoretical contributions rank him with that old but brilliant coterie of Marxist theorists such as Plekhanov, Kautsky, Luxemburg, and for that matter Lenin himself. In addition to his work as theorist there is another element that elevates him above his peers. Trotsky possessed a remarkable prose style, which is exemplified in the excerpt on Fabian Socialism. Magnificent word play, scathing sarcasm, and brilliant character sketches are the hallmarks of his writing. To read Trotsky is to observe the literary artist at work. Stalin's prose compared with Trotsky's is lame, and Lenin's while clear and simple remains nevertheless somewhat pedestrian. Had Trotsky not participated in the tumultuous events of 1905 and 1917, his writings alone would have ensured his reputation as a man of letters.

It is, however, in the realm of practical politics and revolutionary activity that the bizarre element enters his life. Although Trotsky's role in Russian revolutionary history is second only to that of Lenin's, the vast majority of Soviet citizens are unaware of his critical contribution to socialist thought and action. His decisive leadership in the Military Revolutionary Committee that paved the way for the October insurrection and his determined efforts to build the Red Army in the face of enormous obstacles have been wholly blotted from the annals of Soviet history. One reason for this strange turn of events is that Soviet writers have long since abandoned the responsibility of objective historical writing and have busied themselves with the grotesque efforts to create a new demonology. The first rite in the black magic of Soviet historiography was to obliterate any trace of Trotsky's presence. His every action and deed has been expunged from both the written records and the living memory of his compatriots. We are greeted by an awesome silence when we search the official Soviet histories for Trotsky's part in the revolution or the civil war.

The function of this first rite of erasure was the necessary precondition for Trotsky's reappearance as the satanic leader within a new demonic hierarchy. When he reemerges in the writings of Soviet scholars, he no longer bears the qualities of a human being but is presented as an abstraction of evil—a militating force against the future destiny of the Soviet people. And he is not alone, but is surrounded by the lesser demons, particularly the fallen angels of the great purge trials of the 1930s. Together they constitute Trotskyism—a miasmic cloud which hangs over the future of the proletariat. Within the Soviet Union Trotskyism is responsible for every failure, disappointment, or miscalculation. In the world at large Trotskyism is responsible for the rise of fascism, the failure of revolution, and the encirclement of the Soviet Union. The dialectic of history is forced to work in this perverse manner. The documents in Part Two of this book provide us with a necessary antidote—a glimpse of the real Trotsky as he was seen by his contemporaries during those tumultuous days of war and revolution. How differently these eyewitnesses present him in comparison with the negative and bloodless abstraction of official Soviet writing.

Soviet demonology, absurd from its inception, has been largely vanquished, at least in the Western world. Part Three of this book contains selections of relatively recent writers on the problem of Trotsky. The best examples of this more objective scholarship are Edward Hallett Carr's multi-volume study, *The Bolshevik Revolution,* and Isaac Deutscher's painstaking three-volume biography of Trotsky. The historical debate may be never ending, but in the light of these more recent studies Trotsky's role in the Russian experience can be seen in a new and positive perspective. In the West, the miasmic cloud has disappeared; the demonic hierarchy has been exorcized. We can now come to grips with the material forces and issues which motivated and inspired the actions and deeds of Leon Trotsky.

Leon Bronstein was born on a farm called Yanovka in the southern Ukraine, on October 26, 1879, the son of a hard-working and moderately prosperous Jewish farmer. He spent the first nine years of his childhood in this rural backwash, hardly an auspicious background for a future earthshaker. Soon after, his parents sent him to relatives in Odessa, where, in spite of an enforced *numerus clausus* against Jewish students, they hoped he would gain admittance to the St. Paul's *Realschule.* He was successful in his efforts, completed his studies, and eventually entered the Odessa university with the intention of devoting himself to mathematics. Like so many other Russian students, Leon was attracted to the excitement of radical politics and was soon actively engaged in organizing the

Southern Russian Workers Union. His decision made, one can only surmise what mathematics lost, but one can be certain of what radical politics gained. His political involvement rapidly led to his first arrest, and exile to Ust-Kut in Siberia. In the interim he married Alexandra Sokolovskaya, his first wife and an active and dedicated Marxist radical. Within two years he made good his escape, leaving behind his wife and two daughters. It was at this point that he assumed the name of Trotsky.

The following years were to be a whirlwind of activity. Leaving Russia behind he journeyed to England, where he met Lenin and the other members of the editorial staff of *Iskra*. He attended the Second Congress of the Russian Social Democratic Party, within which he eventually broke with Lenin. The break was to lead to long years of estrangement between the two. In Paris he met Natalia Sedova, and though not legally married, they lived together until his death in 1940. They had two sons—Lyova and Sergey. The outbreak of revolution in Russia in 1905 brought them back to St. Petersburg, where Trotsky played a prominent role in the formation of the first Russian soviet. His political reputation was made. With the collapse of the revolution he earned his second arrest and was exiled to Siberia. This time he managed to escape en route and eventually took up residence in Vienna, where he lived until the outbreak of war in 1914. The family then moved to Paris. Trotsky busied himself writing articles and editing a newspaper condemning the imperialist war. French officials considered him a sufficiently dangerous threat to insist on his deportation from France. Embarking from Spain, Trotsky and his family made their way to the United States. They lived a penurious existence in New York until the outbreak of the March Revolution. During this entire period— from his break with Lenin to the outbreak of the war—Trotsky's position was more that of the "loner" in politics. He was equally critical of both Bolsheviks and Mensheviks. It was during the war, however, that he slowly began to gravitate back toward Lenin's position.

As soon as word of the March Revolution spread, Trotsky made preparations to leave New York. His return to Russia was interrupted by one peculiar incident: while travelling he was arrested by British naval authorities and interned in a prisoner-of-war camp in Canada. The Russian Provisional Government interceded on his behalf and he was soon released. His jailers, apparently, were pleased to see him go, since he had made considerable headway in converting German prisoners to the cause of revolution.

For a second time Trotsky was given an opportunity to play a revolutionary role on the stage of history. Shortly after his return to Russia, Lenin invited him to join the Bolshevik Party. Trotsky accepted. For weeks on end Trotsky appeared before large audiences delivering impassioned political speeches denouncing the halfway measures of the Provisional Government, and encouraging crowds of workers to prepare for the overthrow of the regime. Perhaps his greatest achievement was realized when he assumed the leadership of the Military Revolutionary Committee, which was to pave the way for the October insurrection. A story has it that after the Bolsheviks achieved power, Lenin actually proposed that Trotsky should serve as the head of the new government, thus acknowledging his strategic role in bringing success to the revolution. Trotsky refused to accept the honor and instead became the revolution's first Commissar of For- ✕ eign Affairs. Later, Trotsky explained the reason for his refusal to become the head of the new state: apparently he feared that his Jewish origin would be exploited by counterrevolutionists hoping to play upon the anti-Semitic feelings of the masses, and thus turn them against the Bolsheviks.

The Bolsheviks now faced their greatest challenge, as anticommunist forces began to organize serious resistance. Kerensky, the former head of government, boastfully declared that with the assistance of General Krasnov's loyal Cossacks he would soon return to power. Rumors began to circulate that both Lenin and Trotsky had already fled the capital. Again Trotsky demonstrated the versatility of his genius. Amid a situation of incredible chaos he forged the Red Army, which successfully repulsed the Interventionists and defeated the White armies in the civil war. Never in his political career was Trotsky's reputation higher. The names Lenin and Trotsky were inseparably linked in the minds of the Russian masses; yet within a very short period after Lenin's death in 1924, Trotsky's political fortunes began to wane. For seemingly strange and incomprehensible reasons, Trotsky was isolated by the old guard of the party and then abruptly dislodged from power.

The passage of time has helped to place Trotsky's career into clearer perspective. His vital role in the revolution and civil war is recognized, but the reasons for his failures after Lenin's death remain somewhat obscure. A recent writer, attempting a psychoanalytic explanation of Trotsky's be- ⟨ havior, has suggested that the revolutionary personality inevitably experiences acute difficulty once the revolution is achieved. A personality forged by years of active opposition to authority cannot readjust to a new position when it becomes the source of authority. In this sense Trotsky was the eternal revolutionist fated to remain in opposition even after Bolshevik victory.

More material reasons for Trotsky's expulsion from power suggest that, for the greater part of his political career before 1917, he was divorced from any political party and neither owed political allegiance to, nor could expect political support from, a party machine. The fact that Trotsky joined Lenin's party in 1917 did not erase from the minds of stalwart Bolshevik workers his all-too-recent entry. And when the newcomer won Lenin's praise for his brilliant performance, and threatened to become Lenin's eventual successor, their jealousy knew no bounds. "He is with us, but not of us" was the conviction of many in the old guard. And they were quick to rid themselves of a suspected menace.

By strange irony an additional reason for Trotsky's downfall resulted from one of his greatest achievements. The fact that military dictatorship was the final act of the great bourgeois revolutions in England and France remained a matter of great concern to Bolshevik leaders. Repeated references to Cromwell and, moreso, to Napoleon are to be found throughout their writings. Because Trotsky played such an important role as Commissar of War, it was perhaps inevitable that the stranger in their ranks should have been identified as the imminent threat to the revolution—the dreaded "man on horseback." Certainly in the late thirties party members in intimate discussion still spoke of Trotsky as the potential Bonaparte of the revolution.

In retrospect it can be seen that postrevolutionary Russia presented a hostile environment to Trotsky. He appeared to be a displaced person—displaced in time and location. As a man of action he towered over many of his colleagues. His particular forte was demonstrated when he addressed large gatherings and exercised his magic of enchanting the crowds with the desire for revolutionary action. Swift and resolute, he emerged as the natural leader when decisive action had to be taken. But by the mid-twenties the needs of Russia had changed greatly since the days of the civil war. The importance of the Commissariat of War was supplanted by the bureaucracy. The heroism of the battlefield was exchanged for the pedestrian effort to rebuild a shattered economy. And most important, revolutionary camaraderie was replaced by a realignment of political forces within the party, an ominous sign for Trotsky, who was still regarded as the outsider. Evidently he sensed the awkwardness of his position in Russia, because he petitioned the party for permission to move to Germany in order to prepare for the next revolution.

If the times, however, were out of joint the location was equally unpromising. Trotsky was the consummate cosmopolitan. An accomplished linguist, he was equally at home in Paris, London, and Berlin. His philosophy of revolution was predicated on the concept of world revolution; but at that very moment the Russian revolution, the expected forerunner of the final all-embracing revolution, had begun the swift retreat into its own native shell under the slogan of "Socialism in One Country." Trotsky could not settle for the revolution in isolation, and consequently opened himself to the charges of his adversaries that he was an undisciplined adventurer who would jeopardize the Soviet state and everything it stood for.

The sequence of events leading to his ultimate defeat are straightforward: In 1925 he was forced to resign from his post as Commissar of War. In the following year he was deprived of his seat in the Politburo. In 1927 the Central Committee expelled him from the party, and in 1928 he was exiled to Alma-Ata in Soviet Turkestan. Finally, in 1929 he was expelled from the Soviet Union and took up residence on the Turkish island of Prinkipo, where he lived for four years.

The years spent on Prinkipo were fruitful in terms of writing: he completed his autobiography, *My Life,* and the important three-volume study, *History of the Bolshevik Revolution.* He also edited the *Bulletin of the Opposition,* which was to serve for many years as the voice of dissent within the Soviet Union. But it was impossible for Trotsky to remain so far removed from the political nerve centers of the world. In 1933 he finally left the island and took up residence in France. What followed was a story of disappointment and frustration. His reception and treatment in France by both government and right-wing elements were such that he was soon forced to seek refuge elsewhere. In 1935 he settled in Norway, where, it at first appeared, he would be permitted a peaceful life dedicated to study and writing. This, too, soured quickly and he was hounded out of the country. His final destination was Mexico, where he was extended considerable hospitality by the government of President Lazaro Cardenas.

It should be noted that as great as were the hardships and humiliations that Trotsky was forced to endure during his political exile, he remained a staunch defendant of the Soviet Union. Regardless of what he considered to be the abnormal developments within the Soviet Union, he cherished the hope that constructive reforms would eventually eliminate the crude excesses of Stalinism. By the mid-thirties his hopes for reforms began to falter and he finally concluded that only internal revolution would free the toiling masses from the strangling grip of the bureaucracy. Yet he remained emphatic in his insistence that it was the responsibility of all socialists to defend the Soviet Union at any moment of emergency, because it existed as the only example of a workers' state.

By 1940 the acrimonious debate between Stalin and Trotsky had reached such levels of intensity that political assassination became a serious probability. Finally, on August 20, 1940, Trotsky was murdered by a Stalinist agent. In a sense Trotsky's execution was the final scene in the mad drama of Soviet purges of the late thirties.

In 1956 when Khrushchev delivered his blistering attack on Stalin and exposed the brutality and the murders of that period, it became obvious that Soviet historians would soon face the new task of rewriting the past and rehabilitating the victims of Stalinism. The particular event which many observers waited for was the new word on Trotsky. Scores of old-guard Bolsheviks previously condemned as enemies of the people were now exonerated and permitted to take their rightful places in the pantheon of revolutionary heroes. Would Trotsky be accorded the same right?

Almost two decades have elapsed since the Khrushchev revelations, but Trotsky remains the satanic symbol of Soviet historiography. To estimate how long before Soviet officialdom will see fit to dismantle the elaborate system of demonology constructed around Trotsky's name remains a difficult task. But one thing remains certain: Soviet historians will remain incapable of writing the history of the Bolshevik revolution, which is their duty, until they recognize Trotsky's key role in that great event.

Chronology of the Life of Trotsky

1879	(October 26) Lev Bronstein born at Yanovka near the small town of Bobrinetz in the southern Ukraine.
1896	Joins a radical discussion group led by Franz Shvigovsky.
1897	Attends Odessa University and organizes the Southern Russian Workers Union.
1898	Imprisoned in Kherson for political activities.
1899	Sentenced to four years in Ust-Kut, Siberia.
1900	Before deportation marries Alexandra Sokolovskaya. Their daughter Zinaida is born.
1902	Second daughter, Nina, is born. Escapes alone from Siberia and takes the name Trotsky. Reaches London and visits Lenin. Writes his first articles for *Iskra*.
1903	Breaks with Lenin at the second congress of the Russian Social Democratic party. Meets Natalia Sedova in Paris. Although she was referred to as his second wife, they were never legally married.
1905	Returns to Russia to participate in the revolution and plays a leading role in the first Soviet.
1906	The revolution is crushed and he is sentenced to Siberia for life, but escapes while en route and reaches Finland. His son Lyova is born.
1907	Settles in Vienna. Second son, Sergey, is born.
1914	Moves to France at outbreak of war.
1916	Expelled from France, deported to Spain.
1917	Travels to New York with Natalia Sedova and sons. (March 27) Sails from New York for Russia but is arrested by British naval police and is interned at a prisoner-of-war camp in Nova Scotia. (April 29) Released, Trotsky reaches Petrograd May 4 (old calendar). (May 10) Lenin invites Trotsky to join the Bolshevik Party. (September) Trotsky assumes leadership of the Military Revolutionary committee in preparation for the October insurrection. (November) Appointed Commissar of Foreign Affairs of the new Soviet government.
1918	(March) Appointed Commissar of War. Founds the Red Army.

1921   Naval insurrection crushed at Kronstadt on Trotsky's orders.

1924   Death of Lenin. Trotsky publishes his "Lessons of October," which is interpreted by Stalin and the members of the old guard as an attack on themselves.

1925   (January)   Stalin and the Central Committee remove Trotsky from the War Commissariat.
(May)   Appointed to serve on the Supreme Council of the National Economy.

1926   (April)   Trotsky, Kamenev, and Zinoviev form opposition against Stalin within the party.
(October 4)   Trotsky and Zinoviev approach Politburo with proposals for a truce.
(October 18)   Max Eastman publishes Lenin's will in *New York Times*. Stalin, convinced of Trotsky's role, summons the Central Committee (October 23), and deprives Trotsky of his seat in Politburo.

1927   (March 31)   Trotsky attacks Politburo's China policy.
(September 27)   Addresses the Executive Committee of the Comintern for the last time.
(November 14)   Extraordinary session of Central Committee and Central Control Commission expels Trotsky and Zinoviev from the party.
(December 2–9)   Fifteenth Party Congress expels entire Left opposition from the Communist Party.

1928   (January 17)   Deported to Alma-Ata (Turkestan) on charge of counter-revolutionary activity. Daughter Nina dies.

1929   (January)   Exiled from the Soviet Union, Trotsky settles at Prinkipo, a Turkish island in the Sea of Marmara. He remains there for four years. Edits *Bulletin of the Opposition* and completes his *History of the Russian Revolution*.

1932   (February 20)   Deprived of Soviet nationality.

1933   (January)   Learns of his daughter Zina's suicide.
(July)   Receives permission to reside in France.

1935   (June)   Moves to Norway and remains until December, 1936.

1936   Famous Moscow trials. Trotsky and his son Lyova found guilty *in absentia* of directing terrorist acts in Soviet Russia.
Trotsky's younger son, Sergey, arrested and sent to Vorkuta where he died.

1937   (January)   Diego Rivera, the Mexican painter, induces President Cardenas to allow Trotsky to settle in Mexico. Trotsky arrives in Tampico and finally takes up residence in Coyoacan, a suburb of Mexico City.
(April 10)   First meeting of Joint Commission of Inquiry under the chairmanship of John Dewey to refute the charges made against Trotsky in the Moscow trials.

1938   (February 16)   Trotsky's son Lyova dies under mysterious circumstances in France.

(September 3)   Foundation Conference of Trotsky's Fourth International.

1940   (May 23)   Siqueiros, the Mexican artist, leads a machine gun attack on Trotsky's home.

(August 20)   Trotsky assassinated by "Jacson," alias Ramon Mercader.

PART ONE

TROTSKY LOOKS AT THE WORLD

1

The Theorist

Trotsky, the man of action, was also a vigorous and prolific writer. Like Lenin, Trotsky attempted to add, on the basis of his own experience, to the body of Marxist thought. The following two selections are typical examples of his theoretical forays into socio-political problems.

The first selection deals with a question which has been stressed by hostile critics of Marxism. These writers emphasize that among Marxist scholars it was axiomatic to expect the socialist revolution to occur first in the most advanced capitalist societies, i.e., where capitalism had performed its necessary function of creating both a complex industrial base and an army of proletarian workers, who, having attained the necessary level of political consciousness, would then overthrow the capitalist system. Contrary to these expectations, the revolution did not come to England, Germany, or France but to the most backward of the large European powers—Czarist Russia. This fact alone is presented as sufficient evidence of the weakness in Marxist thought. It was the Russian revolution of 1905 which forced Trotsky to re-examine the supposed discrepancy between Marxist theory and historical event.

The second selection deals with Trotsky's concept of permanent revolution. According to this, revolutions transforming backward societies would have to be enormously telescoped in time, moving in almost uninterrupted fashion from feudal to bourgeois and ultimately socialist society. In addition, the theory suggested that the socialist revolution could not be contained within the frame of an isolated state but would have to spread rapidly throughout the capitalist world. It was this particular contribution of Trotsky which led to the sharpest encounters with Stalin in the mid-twenties.

PREREQUISITES OF REVOLUTION[1]

. . . The proletariat grows and gains strength with the growth of capitalism. From this viewpoint, the development of capitalism is the development of the proletariat for dictatorship. The day and the hour, however, when political power should pass into the hands of the working class, is determined not directly by the degree of capitalistic development of economic forces, but by the relations of class struggle, by the international situation, by a number of subjective elements, such as tradition, initiative, readiness to fight. . . .

It is, therefore, not excluded that in a backward country with a lesser degree of capitalistic development, the proletariat should sooner reach political supremacy than in a highly developed capitalist state. Thus, in middle-class Paris, the proletariat consciously took into its hands the administration of public affairs in 1871. True it is, that the reign of the proletariat lasted only for two months, it is remarkable, however, that in far more advanced capitalist centers of England and the United States, the proletariat never was in power even for the duration of one day. To imagine that there is an automatic dependence between a dictatorship of the proletariat — and the technical and productive resources of a country, is to understand economic determinism in a very primitive way. Such a conception would have nothing to do with Marxism.

It is our opinion that the Russian revolution creates conditions whereby political power can (and, in case of a victorious revolution, *must*) pass into the hands of the proletariat before the politicians of the liberal bourgeoisie would have occasion to give their political genius full swing.

Summing up the results of the revolution and counter-revolution in 1848 and 1849, Marx wrote in his correspondences to the New York *Tribune*: "The working class in Germany is, in its social and political development, as far behind that of England and France as the German bourgeoisie is behind the bourgeoisie of these countries. Like master, like man. The evolution of the conditions of existence for a numerous, strong, concentrated, and intelligent proletariat goes hand in hand with the development of the conditions of existence for a numerous, wealthy, concentrated and powerful middle class. The working class movement itself never is inde-

[1] From Leon Trotsky, *Our Revolution*, trans. by Moissaye J. Olgin (New York: Holt, Rinehart Co., 1918), pp. 84–91, 119–123. All rights reserved. Reprinted by permission of Holt, Rinehart and Winston, Inc.

pendent, never is of an exclusively proletarian character until all the different factions of the middle class, and particularly its most progressive faction, the large manufacturers, have conquered political power, and remodeled the State according to their wants. It is then that the inevitable conflict between employer and the employed becomes imminent, and cannot be adjourned any longer." This quotation must be familiar to the reader, as it has lately been very much abused by scholastic Marxists. It has been used as an iron-clad argument against the idea of a labor government in Russia. If the Russian capitalistic bourgeoisie is not strong enough to take governmental power into its hands, how is it possible to think of an industrial democracy, i.e., a political supremacy of the proletariat, was the question.

Let us give this objection closer consideration.

Marxism is primarily a method of analysis,—not the analysis of texts, but the analysis of social relations. Applied to Russia, is it true that the weakness of capitalistic liberalism means the weakness of the working class? Is it true, not in the abstract, but in relation to Russia, that an independent proletarian movement is impossible before the bourgeoisie assume political power? It is enough to formulate these questions in order to understand what hopeless logical formalism there is hidden behind the attempt to turn Marx's historically relative remark into a super-historic maxim.

Our industrial development, though marked in times of prosperity by leaps and bounds of an "American" character, is in reality miserably small in comparison with the industry of the United States. Five million persons, forming 16.6 per cent of the population engaged in economic pursuits, are employed in the industries of Russia; six millions and 22.2 per cent are the corresponding figures for the United States. To have a clear idea as to the real dimensions of industry in both countries, we must remember that the population of Russia is twice as large as the population of the United States, and that the output of American industries in 1900 amounted to 25 billions of rubles whereas the output of Russian industries for the same year hardly reached 2.5 billions.

There is no doubt that the number of the proletariat, the degree of its concentration, its cultural level, and its political importance depend upon the degree of industrial development in each country.

This dependence, however, is not a direct one. Between the productive forces of a country on one side and the political strength of its social classes on the other, there is at any given moment a current and cross current of various socio-political factors of a national and international character which modify and sometimes completely reverse the political expression of economic relations. The industry of the United States is far more advanced than the industry of Russia, while the political role of the Russian workingmen, their influence on the political life of their country, the possibilities of their influence on world politics in the near future, are incomparably greater than those of the American proletariat.

In his recent work on the American workingman, Kautsky arrives at the conclusion that there is no immediate and direct dependence between the political strength of the bourgeoisie and the proletariat of a country on one hand and its industrial development on the other. "Here are two countries," he writes, "diametrically opposed to each other: in one of them, one of the elements of modern industry is developed out of proportion, i.e., out of keeping with the stage of capitalistic development; in the other, another; in America it is the class of capitalists; in Russia, the class of labor. In America there is more ground than elsewhere to speak of the dictatorship of capital, while nowhere has labor gained as much influence as in Russia, and this influence is bound to grow, as Russia has only recently entered the period of modern class struggle." Kautsky then proceeds to state that Germany can, to a certain degree, study her future from the present conditions in Russia, then he continues: "It is strange to think that it is the Russian proletariat which shows us our future as far as, not the organization of capital, but the protest of the working class is concerned. Russia is the most backward of all the great states of the capitalist world. This may seem to be in contradiction with the economic interpretation of history which considers economic strength the basis of political development. This is, however, not true. It contradicts only that kind of economic interpretation of history which is being painted by our opponents and critics who see in it not *a method of analysis,* but *a ready pattern.*" These lines ought to be recommended to those of our native Marxians who substitute for an independent analysis of social relations a deduction from texts selected for all emergencies of life. No one can compromise Marxism as shamefully as these bureaucrats of Marxism do.

In Kautsky's estimation, Russia is characterized, economically, by a comparatively low level of capitalistic development; politically, by a weakness of the capitalistic bourgeoisie and by a great strength of the working class. This results in the fact, that "the struggle for the interests of Russia as a whole has become the task of the only powerful class in Russia, industrial labor. This is the reason why labor has gained such a tremendous political importance. This is the reason why the struggle of Russia against the polyp of absolutism which is strangling the country, turned out to be a single combat where the peasantry can lend considerable assistance without, however, being able to play a leading role.

Are we not warranted in our conclusion that the "man" will sooner gain political supremacy in Russia than his "master"?

. . . To make Socialism possible, a social power has to arise in the midst of the antagonistic classes of capitalist society, a power objectively placed in a position to be interested in the establishment of Socialism, at the same time strong enough to overcome all opposing interests and hostile resistance. It is one of the principal merits of scientific Socialism to have discovered such a social power in the person of the proletariat, and to have shown that this class, growing with the growth of capitalism, can find its salvation only in Socialism; that it is being moved towards Socialism by its very position, and that the doctrine of Socialism in the presence of a capitalist society must necessarily become the ideology of the proletariat.

How far, then, must the social differentiation have gone to warrant the assertion that the second prerequisite is an accomplished fact? In other words, what must be the numerical strength of the proletariat? Must it be one-half, two-thirds, or nine-tenths of the people? It is utterly futile to try and formulate this second prerequisite of Socialism arithmetically. An attempt to express the strength of the proletariat in mere numbers, besides being schematic, would imply a series of difficulties. Whom should we consider a proletarian? Is the half-paupered peasant a proletarian? Should we count with the proletariat those hosts of the city reserve who, on one hand, fall into the ranks of the parasitic proletariat of beggars and thieves, and, on the other hand, fill the streets in the capacity of peddlers, i.e., of parasites on the economic body as a whole? It is not easy to answer these questions.

The importance of the proletariat is based not only on its numbers, but primarily on its role in industry. The political supremacy of the bourgeoisie is founded on economic power. Before it manages to take over the authority of the state, it concentrates in its hands the national means of production; hence its specific weight. The proletariat will possess no means of production of its own before the Social revolution. Its social power depends upon the circumstance that the means of production in possession of the bourgeoisie can be put into motion only by the hands of the proletariat. From the bourgeois viewpoint, the proletariat is also one of the means of production, forming, in combination with the others, a unified mechanism. Yet the proletariat is the only non-automatic part of this mechanism, and can never be made automatic, notwithstanding all efforts. This puts the proletariat into a position to be able to stop the functioning of the national economic body, partially or wholly—through the medium of partial or general strikes.

Hence it is evident that, the numerical strength of the proletariat being equal, its importance is proportional to the mass of the means of production it puts into motion: the proletarian of a big industrial concern represents—other conditions being equal—a greater social unit than an artisan's employee; a city workingman represents a greater unit than a proletarian of the village. In other words, the political role of the proletariat is greater in proportion as large industries predominate over small industries, industry predominates over agriculture, and the city over the village.

At a period in the history of Germany or England when the proletariats of those countries formed the same percentage to the total population as the proletariat in present-day Russia, they did not possess the same social weight as the Russian proletariat of to-day. They could not possess it, because their objective importance in economic life was comparatively smaller. The social weight of the cities represents the same phenomenon. At a time when the city population of Germany formed only 15 per cent of the total nation, as is the case in present-day Russia, the German cities were far from equaling our cities in economic and political importance. The concentration of big industries and commercial enterprises in the cities, and the establishment of closer relations between city and country through a system of railways, has given the modern cities an importance far exceeding the mere volume of their population. Moreover, the growth of their importance runs ahead of the growth of their population, and the growth of the latter runs ahead of the natural increase of the entire population of the country. In 1848, the number of artisans, masters and their employees, in Italy was 15 per cent of the population, the same as the percentage of the proletariat, including artisans, in Russia of to-day. Their importance, however, was far less than that of the Russian industrial proletariat.

The question is not, how strong the proletariat is numerically, but what is its position in the general economy of a country.

PERMANENT REVOLUTION [2]

I hope that the reader will not object if, to end this book, I attempt, without fear of repetition, to formulate succinctly my principal conclusions.

1. The theory of the permanent revolution now demands the greatest attention from every Marxist, for the course of the class and ideological struggle has fully and finally raised this question from the realm of reminiscences over old differences of opinion among Russian Marxists, and converted it into a question of the character, the inner connexions and methods of the international revolution in general.

2. With regard to countries with a belated bourgeois development, especially the colonial and semi-colonial countries, the theory of the permanent revolution signifies that the complete and genuine solution of their tasks of achieving *democracy and national emancipation* is conceivable only through the dictatorship of the proletariat as the leader of the subjugated nation, above all of its peasant masses.

3. Not only the agrarian, but also the national question assigns to the peasantry—the overwhelming majority of the population in backward countries—an exceptional place in the democratic revolution. Without an alliance of the proletariat with the peasantry the tasks of the democratic revolution cannot be solved, nor even seriously posed. But the alliance of these two classes can be realized in no other way than through an irreconcilable struggle against the influence of the national-liberal bourgeoisie.

4. No matter what the first episodic stages of the revolution may be in the individual countries, the realization of the revolutionary alliance between the proletariat and the peasantry is conceivable only under the political leadership of the proletarian vanguard, organized in the Communist Party. This in turn means that the victory of the democratic revolution is conceivable only through the dictatorship of the proletariat which bases itself upon the alli-

[2] From Leon Trotsky, *The Permanent Revolution* (New York: Pathfinder Press, 1970), pp. 276–81. Reprinted by permission of the publisher.

ance with the peasantry and solves first of all the tasks of the democratic revolution.

5. Assessed historically, the old slogan of Bolshevism—"the democratic dictatorship of the proletariat and peasantry"—expressed precisely the above-characterized relationship of the proletariat, the peasantry and the liberal bourgeoisie. This has been confirmed by the experience of October. But Lenin's old formula did not settle in advance the problem of what the reciprocal relations would be between the proletariat and the peasantry within the revolutionary bloc. In other words, the formula deliberately retained a certain algebraic quality, which had to make way for more precise arithmetical quantities in the process of historical experience. However, the latter showed, and under circumstances that exclude any kind of misinterpretation, that no matter how great the revolutionary role of the peasantry may be, it nevertheless cannot be an independent role and even less a leading one. The peasant follows either the worker or the bourgeois. This means that the "democratic dictatorship of the proletariat and peasantry" is only conceivable as a *dictatorship of the proletariat that leads the peasant masses behind it.*

6. A democratic dictatorship of the proletariat and peasantry, as a regime that is distinguished from the dictatorship of the proletariat by its class content, might be realized only in a case where an *independent* revolutionary party could be constituted, expressing the interests of the peasants and in general of petty-bourgeois democracy—a party capable of conquering power with this or that degree of aid from the proletariat, and of determining its revolutionary programme. As all modern history attests—especially the Russian experience of the last twenty-five years—an insurmountable obstacle on the road to the creation of a peasants' party is the petty-bourgeoisie's lack of economic and political independence and its deep internal differentiation. By reason of this the upper sections of the petty-bourgeoisie (of the peasantry) go along with the big bourgeoisie in all decisive cases, especially in war and in revolution; the lower sections go along with the proletariat; the intermediate section being thus compelled to choose between the two extreme poles. Between Kerenskyism and the Bolshevik power, between the Kuomintang and the dictatorship of the proletariat, there is not and cannot be any intermediate stage, that is, no democratic dictatorship of the workers and peasants.

7. The Comintern's endeavour to foist upon the Eastern coun-

tries the slogan of the democratic dictatorship of the proletariat and peasantry, finally and long ago exhausted by history, can have only a reactionary effect. Insofar as this slogan is counterposed to the slogan of the dictatorship of the proletariat, it contributes politically to the dissolution of the proletariat in the petty-bourgeois masses and thus creates the most favourable conditions for the hegemony of the national bourgeoisie and consequently for the collapse of the democratic revolution. The introduction of this slogan into the programme of the Comintern is a direct betrayal of Marxism and of the October tradition of Bolshevism.

8. The dictatorship of the proletariat which has risen to power as the leader of the democratic revolution is inevitably and very quickly confronted with tasks, the fulfilment of which is bound up with deep inroads into the rights of bourgeois property. The democratic revolution grows over directly into the socialist revolution and thereby becomes a *permanent* revolution.

9. The conquest of power by the proletariat does not complete the revolution, but only opens it. Socialist construction is conceivable only on the foundation of the class struggle, on a national and international scale. This struggle, under the conditions of an overwhelming predominance of capitalist relationships on the world arena, must inevitably lead to explosions, that is, internally to civil wars and externally to revolutionary wars. Therein lies the permanent character of the socialist revolution as such, regardless of whether it is a backward country that is involved, which only yesterday accomplished its democratic revolution, or an old capitalist country which already has behind it a long epoch of democracy and parliamentarism.

10. The completion of the socialist revolution within national limits is unthinkable. One of the basic reasons for the crisis in bourgeois society is the fact that the productive forces created by it can no longer be reconciled with the framework of the national state. From this follow, on the one hand, imperialist wars, on the other, the utopia of a bourgeois United States of Europe. The socialist revolution begins on the national arena, it unfolds on the international arena, and is completed on the world arena. Thus, the socialist revolution becomes a permanent revolution in a newer and broader sense of the word; it attains completion only in the final victory of the new society on our entire planet.

11. The above-outlined sketch of the development of the world revolution eliminates the question of countries that are 'mature' or

'immature' for socialism in the spirit of that pedantic, lifeless classi-
fication given by the present programme of the Comintern. Insofar
as capitalism has created a world market, a world division of labour
and world productive forces, it has also prepared world economy as
a whole for socialist transformation.

Different countries will go through this process at different tempos.
Backward countries may, under certain conditions, arrive at the
dictatorship of the proletariat sooner than advanced countries, but
they will come later than the latter to socialism.

A backward colonial or semi-colonial country, the proletariat of
which is insufficiently prepared to unite the peasantry and take
power, is thereby incapable of bringing the democratic revolution
to its conclusion. Contrariwise, in a country where the proletariat
has power in its hands as the result of the democratic revolution,
the subsequent fate of the dictatorship and socialism depends in the
last analysis not only and not so much upon the national productive
forces as upon the development of the international socialist revolution.

12. The theory of socialism in one country, which rose on the
yeast of the reaction against October, is the only theory that consistently and to the very end opposes the theory of the permanent
revolution.

The attempt of the epigones, under the lash of our criticism, to
confine the application of the theory of socialism in one country
exclusively to Russia, because of its specific characteristics (its
vastness and its natural resources), does not improve matters but
only makes them worse. The break with the internationalist position
always and invariably leads to national *messianism,* that is, to attributing special superiorities and qualities to one's own country,
which allegedly permit it to play a role to which other countries
cannot attain.

The world division of labour, the dependence of Soviet industry
upon foreign technology, the dependence of the productive forces
of the advanced countries of Europe upon Asiatic raw materials,
etc., etc., make the construction of an independent socialist society
in any single country in the world impossible.

13. The theory of Stalin and Bukharin, running counter to the
entire experience of the Russian revolution, not only sets up the
democratic revolution mechanically in contrast to the socialist revolution, but also makes a breach between the national revolution
and the international revoluton.

This theory imposes upon revolutions in backward countries the task of establishing an unrealizable regime of democratic dictatorship, which it counterposes to the dictatorship of the proletariat. Thereby this theory introduces illusions and fictions into politics, paralyses the struggle for power of the proletariat in the East, and hampers the victory of the colonial revolution.

The very seizure of power by the proletariat signifies, from the standpoint of the epigones' theory, the completion of the revolution ('to the extent of nine-tenths,' according to Stalin's formula) and the opening of the epoch of national reforms. The theory of the kulak growing into socialism and the theory of the 'neutralization' of the world bourgeoisie are consequently inseparable from the theory of socialism in one country. They stand or fall together.

By the theory of national socialism, the Communist International is down-graded to an auxiliary weapon useful only for the struggle against military intervention. The present policy of the Comintern, its regime and the selection of its leading personnel correspond entirely to the demotion of the Communist International to the role of an auxiliary unit which is not destined to solve independent tasks.

14. The programme of the Comintern created by Bukharin is eclectic through and through. It makes the hopeless attempt to reconcile the theory of socialism in one country with Marxist internationalism, which is, however, inseparable from the permanent character of the world revolution. The struggle of the Communist Left Opposition for a correct policy and a healthy regime in the Communist International is inseparably bound up with the struggle for the Marxist programme. The question of the programme is in turn inseparable from the question of the two mutually exclusive theories: the theory of permanent revolution and the theory of socialism in one country. The problem of the permanent revolution has long ago outgrown the episodic differences of opinion between Lenin and Trotsky, which were completely exhausted by history. The struggle is between the basic ideas of Marx and Lenin on the one side and the eclecticism of the centrists on the other.

2

Political Analyst
and Commentator

Trotsky's writings reflect his international interests. He did not confine his literary work to the Russian scene but wrote on a host of problems, including Fabian socialism, American imperialism, Fascism, The New Deal, and countless other topics. The following excerpts reveal Trotsky at his best, a combination of vitriolic humor and penetrating insight.

FABIAN SOCIALISM [1]

MacDonald is opposed to revolution, but he is in favor of organic evolution: he applies to society a few badly digested biological conceptions. Revolution for him, as a sum of cumulative partial changes, is similar to the evolution of living organisms, such as that which transforms the larva into a butterfly; and furthermore, in this latter process, he overlooks precisely the decisively critical moment when the new animal breaks through the old envelope by the method of revolution. It may be observed, by the way, that MacDonald is "in favor of a revolution like that which went on in the bowels of feudalism, when the industrial revolution was maturing." In his boundless ignorance MacDonald apparently imagines that the industrial revolution proceeded as a molecular process, without upheavals, without devastation. He simply does not know the history of England, not to speak of the history of other countries. And he above all does not understand that the industrial revolution, which had been maturing in the womb of feudalism in the form of the accumulation of commercial capital, led to the Reformation, brought the Stuarts into conflict with Parliament, gave birth to the Great Rebellion, laid England waste and bare—in order later to enrich the country.

It would be too boring to dwell here on an interpretation of the

[1] From Leon Trotsky, *Whither England?* (New York: International Publishers, 1925), pp. 80–91.

process of the transformation from the larva into the butterfly, with the object of obtaining the necessary social analogies. It is perhaps simpler and more speedy to recommend to MacDonald to ponder on the time-honored comparison of revolution with the process of birth. Should we not learn a "lesson" from birth, as from the Russian Revolution? In birth also, there is "nothing" but agony and travail (of course, the baby does not count!). Should we not recommend the populace of the future to multiply by painless Fabian methods, by resorting to the talents of Mrs. Snowden as a midwife?

Of course, we are aware that the matter is not altogether a simple one. Even the chicken which is growing in the egg must apply force in order to break its calcareous prison; if any Fabian chicken should refrain—for Christian or other considerations—from this application of force, it would be choked by its hard shell of lime. English pigeon-fanciers, by a method of artificial selection, have succeeded in producing a variety by a progressive shortening of the bill. They have even gone so far as to attain a form in which the bill of the new scion is so short that the poor creature is incapable of breaking through the shell of the egg in which it is born. The unhappy pigeon perishes, a victim of its compulsory abstention from the use of force, and the further progress of the variety of short-billed pigeons is thus terminated. If our memory does not deceive us, MacDonald may read up on this matter in his Darwin. Having been induced to enter the path of analogy with the organic world, which is such a hobby with MacDonald, we may say that the political skill of the English bourgeoisie consists in shortening the revolutionary bill of the proletariat and thus preventing them from breaking through the shell of the capitalist state. The bill of the proletariat is its party. A single glance at MacDonald, (James Henry) Thomas, Mr. and Mrs. Snowden, is sufficient to convince us that the work of the bourgeoisie in the selection of short-billed and soft-billed specimens has been crowned with immense success, for these ladies and gentlemen are not only not fit for breaking through the shell of the capitalist system, but are good for nothing whatsoever.

But here the analogy ends, and reveals the disadvantage of basing one's argument on scattered facts obtained from textbooks of biology rather than on the scientific conditions and stages of historical development. Human society, although growing out of the conditions of the organic and inorganic world, is nevertheless so complicated and concentrated a combination of these conditions as to demand independent study. The social organism differs from the biological organism, for instance, in its much greater elasticity, adaptability of the elements for regrouping, for a (to a certain extent) conscious selection of their tools and methods, for a (within certain limits) conscious utilization of the experience of the past, etc. The little pigeon in its egg cannot change its short bill for a longer one, and therefore perishes. But the working class, when faced with the question "to be or not to be" will discard MacDonald and Mrs. Snowden and equip itself with the beak of a revolutionary party for the overthrow of the capitalist system.

It is particularly interesting to observe in MacDonald a combination of a crassly biological theory of society with an idealistic Christian hatred of materialism. "You speak of revolution, of catastrophic changes, but look at nature; how wise is the action of the caterpillar when it envelops itself in the cocoon; look at the worthy tortoise, and you will find in its movements the natural rhythm for the transformation of society. Learn from nature!" In the same spirit MacDonald brands materialism as a "vulgar, senseless claim, without any spiritual or mental delicacy." . . . MacDonald and delicacy! Is it not an astonishing "delicacy" which seeks inspiration in the caterpillar for the collective social activity of man and simultaneously demands for its own private use an immortal soul and all the comforts of life in the here-after?

"Socialists are accused of being poets. That is true," MacDonald explains, "we are poets. There is no fine policy without poetry. In fact, without poetry there is nothing fine." And so forth, all in the same style, until, at the conclusion: "Above all, the world needs a political and social Shakespeare." This prattle about poetry may be politically not quite so silly as the remarks on the inadmissibility of force. But the full lack of inspiration in MacDonald is here expressed even more strongly, if that were possible. The dull and timid miser in whom there is as much poetry as in a square end of felt, tries to impress the world with his Shakespearean antics. Here you will really find the "monkey pranks" which MacDonald would like to ascribe to the Bolsheviks.

MacDonald, the "poet" of Fabianism! The policy of Sidney Webb, an artistic creation! The Thomas Ministry, colonial poetry! And finally, Mr. Snowden's budget, a triumphant love song of the City (London's financial district)!

While babbling about his social Shakespeare, MacDonald overlooks Lenin. It is an excellent thing for MacDonald—though not for Shakespeare—that the great English poet produced his creations more than three centuries ago; MacDonald has had sufficient time to appreciate Shakespeare as Shakespeare. He would never have recognized him had Shakespeare been one of his contemporaries. So Mac-Donald ignores—completely and definitely ignores—Lenin. The blindness of the Philistine finds its dual expression in pointless sighs for Shakespeare and in a failure to appreciate his most powerful contemporary.

"Socialism is interested in art and in the classics." It is surprising how this "poet" can corrupt by his mere touch thoughts that have nothing inherently vile about them. To convince himself of this, the reader need only read the inference: "Even where there exists great poverty and great unemployment, as is unfortunately the case in our country, citizens (?) should not deny themselves the purchase of paintings or of anything, in general, that may call forth joy and improve the minds of young and old." This excellent advice does not make it entirely clear, however, whether the purchase of paintings is recommended to the unemployed themselves, with the implication that the necessary supplementary appropriations will be made for this need, or whether MacDonald is advising wellborn gentlemen and ladies to purchase paintings "in spite of unemployment" and thus to "improve their minds." We may assume that the second explanation is the correct one. But then, we are constrained to behold in MacDonald a priest of the parlor-Liberal Protestant school, who first speaks with powerful words of poverty and the "religion of conscience" and then advises his worldly flock not to surrender too much to despair and to continue their former mode of living. Let him who will—after this—believe that materialism is vulgarity and that MacDonald is a social poet, languishing with longing for a Shakespeare. As for us, we believe that, if there is in the physical world an absolute zero, corresponding to the greatest attainable cold, there is also in the mental world a degree of absolute vulgarity, corresponding to the mental temperature of Mac-Donald.

Sidney and Beatrice Webb represent a different variety of Fabianism. They are accustomed to patient and laborious literary labor, know the value of facts and figures, and this circumstance imposes certain limitations on their diffuse thought. They are not less boring than MacDonald, but they may be more instructive when they do not attempt to transcend the bounds of investigations of fact. In the domain of generalization they are hardly superior to Mac-

Donald. At the 1923 congress of the Labour Party, Sidney Webb declared that the founder of British socialism was not Karl Marx but Robert Owen, who did not preach the class struggle but the time-honored doctrine of the brotherhood of all mankind. Sidney Webb still considers John Mill a classic of political economy and accordingly teaches that the struggle should be carried on not between capital and labor but between the overwhelming majority of the nation and the expropriators of rents. This should be sufficient to indicate the theoretical level of the principal economist of the Labour Party! The historical process, as we all know, does not proceed according to Webb's desires, even in England. The trade unions are organizations of wage labor against capital. On the basis of the trade unions we have the growth of the Labour Party, which even made Sidney Webb a cabinet minister. Webb carried out his platform only in the sense that he waged no war against the expropriators of surplus value. But he waged no war either against the expropriators of rents.

In 1923, the Webbs issued a book, *The Decay of Capitalist Civilization,* which has as its basis a partly outgrown, partly refurbished paraphrase of Kautsky's old commentaries on the Erfurt Program. But the political tendency of Fabianism is again revealed in *The Decay of Capitalist Civilization* in all its hopelessness, this time half-knowingly. There is no doubt (for whom?) say the Webbs, that the capitalist system will change. The whole question simply is how it is to be transformed. "It may by considerate adaptation be made to pass gradually and peacefully into a new form." But this requires a certain element: good will on both sides. "Unfortunately," the respected authors relate, "many who assent to this proposition of inevitable change, fail to realize what the social institutions are to which this law of change applies. To them the basis of all possible civilization is private property in a sense in which it is so bound up with human nature, that whilst men remain men, it is no more capable of decay or supersession than the rotation of the earth on its axis. But they misunderstand the position." How unhappily have circumstances conspired to frustrate us! The whole business could be arranged to the general satisfaction by applying a method of "planful adaptation," if the workers and capitalists could only agree on the method of this consummation. But since no such agreement has "hitherto" been attained, the capitalists vote for the Conservatives. What should be our conclusion? Here our poor Fabians fail us completely, and here *The Decay of Capitalist Civilization* assumes the form of a lamentable decay of Fabianism. "Before the Great War there seemed to be a substantial measure of consent," the book relates, "that the social order had to be gradually changed, in the direction of a greater equality, etc." By whom was this recognized? These people think their little Fabian molehill is the universe. "We thought, perhaps wrongly (!), that this characteristic British (?) acquiescence on the part of a limited governing class in the rising claims of those who had found themselves excluded from both enjoyment and control, would continue and be extended, willingly or reluctantly, still further from the political into the industrial sphere; and that while progress might be slow, there would at least be no reaction. But after the War, everything fell into desuetude: the conditions of the lives of the workers became worse, we are threatened with the reestablishment of the *veto* power of the House of Lords, with the particular object of resisting further 'concessions to the worker,' " etc. What is the conclusion to be drawn from all this? It was in their hopeless search for such a conclusion that the Webbs wrote their little book. Its final sentence reads as follows: "In an attempt, *possibly vain,* to make the parties understand their problems and each other better—in the hope that it is not always inevitable that Nature should harden the hearts of those whom she intends to destroy—we offer this little book." Is not this nice: a "little book" is offered as a means of conciliating the proletariat with the bourgeoisie. Let us recapitulate: before the war, "it seemed" to be generally recognized that the present system must be altered for the better; however, there was no general agreement as to the character of this change: the capitalists stood for private property, the workers against private property; after the war, the objective situation became worse, and the political divergence became further aggravated; *therefore,* the Webbs write a little book in order to make both sides more inclined toward conciliation; but this hope is admitted to be "possibly vain." Yes, possibly, quite possibly. The worthy Webbs, who are so strongly imbued with a faith in the powers of intellectual conviction, ought—it appears to us—in the interest of "gradual changes," to apply themselves, at least at the beginning to a simpler task, namely, that of persuading a few high-placed Christian scoundrels to renounce their monopoly in the opium trade and their poisoning of millions of people in the Orient.

Oh, how poor, base, weak-minded, how vile in its intellectual cowardice is this Fabianism!

It is entirely impossible to attempt to enumerate all the philosophical varieties of Fabianism, for among this class "liberty of opinion" prevails in the sense that each of its leaders has his own personal philosophy, which consists, in the last analysis, of the same reactionary elements of Conservatism, Liberalism, and Protestantism as in any other such combination. Not long ago, we were very much surprised to learn that so ingenious—we had thought—and so critical a writer as George Bernard Shaw had advised us that Marx had been far surpassed by (H. G.) Wells's great work on history.[2] These revelations, an entire surprise to all of mankind, may be explained by the fact that the Fabians constitute from the standpoint of theory, an absolutely closed microcosm of profoundly provincial nature, in spite of the fact that they live in London. Their philosophical excogitations are apparently of no use either to Conservatives or to Liberals. They are of still less use to the working class, to whom they neither give nor explain anything. Their productions serve in the last analysis only to make clear to the Fabians themselves what is the use of the existence of Fabianism. Together with theological literature, these works seem to be the most useless, at any rate, the most boring, form of intellectual creation.

At present it is customary in England in certain fields of activity to speak with a certain contempt of the men of the "Victorian era," i.e., the outstanding figures of the time of Queen Victoria. Everything has changed since then in England, but the Fabian type has perhaps been preserved even more intact. The insipid, optimistic Victorian epoch, in which it was believed that tomorrow will be somewhat better than today and the day after tomorrow still better than tomorrow, has found its most perfect expression in the Webbs, Snowden, MacDonald, and other Fabians. They may therefore be considered as an awkward and useless survival of an epoch that has already been definitely and irrevocably destroyed. We may say without exaggeration, that the Fabian Society, founded in 1884, with the object of "awakening the social consciousness," is now the

---

[2] I regret to say that before I read Shaw's letter, I had not even known of the existence of Wells's *Outline of History*. I later became acquainted with it; conscience prevents me from saying that I read it through, for an acquaintance with two or three chapters was quite sufficient to induce me to desist from a further waste of time. Imagine an absolute absence of method, of historical perspective, of understanding of the mutual dependence of the various phases of social life; in general, of any kind of scientific discipline; and then imagine the "historian" burdened with these accomplishments, with the carefree mind of a Sunday pedestrian, strolling aimlessly and awkwardly through a few thousand years of history, and then you have Wells's book, which is to replace the Marxian school.

most reactionary group to be found in Great Britain. Neither the Conservative clubs nor Oxford University, nor the higher Anglican clergy nor other priestly institutions, can begin to be compared with the Fabians. For all these are institutions of our enemies, and the revolutionary movement of the proletariat will inevitably break down their walls. But the proletariat is being restrained precisely by its own leading ranks, i.e., by the Fabian politicians and their mental offspring. These inflated authorities, pedants, conceited and highfalutin cowards are systematically poisoning the labor movement, obscuring the consciousness of the proletariat, paralyzing its will. Thanks only to them, Toryism, Liberalism, the Church, the monarchy, the aristocracy, the bourgeoisie, continue to maintain themselves and even to feel secure in the saddle. The Fabians, the Independents, the conservative bureaucracy of the trade unions, are now the most counterrevolutionary power in Great Britain and perhaps in the entire present stage of the world situation. The driving out of the Fabians will be equivalent to a liberation of the revolutionary energy of the proletariat of Great Britain, to Socialism's conquest of the British fortress of reaction, to the freeing of India and Egypt, and to a mighty stimulus to the movement and growth of the peoples of the Orient. Renouncing force, the Fabians believe only in the power of "ideas." The kernel of truth imprisoned by this vile, hypocritical philosophy is merely the fact that no system can be maintained by force alone. And this holds good also of the British imperialist system. In a country in which the overwhelming majority of the population consists of proletarians, the ruling Conservative-Liberal imperialist clique could not have maintained itself for a single day if the instruments of force which this clique holds in its hands were not reinforced, supplemented, and coated with pseudo-Socialist ideals, confusing and disintegrating the proletariat.

The French "enlighteners" of the eighteenth century considered Catholicism, clericalism, the priesthood, to be their great enemy, and felt it was necessary to *écraser l'infâme* (crush the infamous), before further progress was possible. They were right in the sense that it was the priesthood, the organized system of superstition, of the Catholic mental police system, which stood in the way of bourgeois society, obstructing the growth of science, art, political ideas, economics. Fabianism, MacDonaldism, pacifism, now play precisely the same role in relation to the historical movement of the proletariat. Fabianism is the chief support of British and European imperialism, if not of the entire world bourgeoisie; we must point out to the workers the true countenance of these self-complacent pedants, prattling eclectics, sentimental careerists, liveried footmen of the bourgeoisie. In showing them up for what they are, we are discrediting them forever. In discrediting them, we are performing an immense service to historical progress. On the day when the English proletariat frees itself from the mental baseness of Fabianism, humanity, particularly in Europe, will increase in stature by at least a head.

3
Critic of the Soviet Experience

Expelled from the Soviet Union in 1929, Trotsky spent much of his time observing Russian developments from afar. It would be no exaggeration to state that he was preoccupied with such questions as: How did the bureaucracy attain control of party and people? How did Stalin triumph? Had the revolution been overtaken by the Thermidorian reaction? The following excerpt is Trotsky's attempt to answer these profound questions.

REVOLUTION PERVERTED [1]

The historian of the Soviet Union cannot fail to conclude that the policy of the ruling bureaucracy upon great questions has been a series of contradictory zigzags. The attempt to explain or justify them by "changing circumstances" obviously won't hold water. To guide means at least in some degree to exercise foresight. The Stalin faction have not in the slightest degree foreseen the inevitable results of the development; they have been caught napping every time. They have reacted with mere administrative reflexes. The theory of each successive turn has been created after the fact, and with small regard for what they were teaching yesterday. On the basis of the same irrefutable facts and documents, the historian will be compelled to conclude that the so-called "Left-Opposition" offered an immeasurably more correct analysis of the processes taking place in the country, and far more truly foresaw their further development.

This assertion is contradicted at first glance by the simple fact that the faction which could not see ahead was steadily victorious, while the more penetrating group suffered defeat after defeat. That kind of objection, which comes automatically to mind, is convincing, however, only for those who think rationalistically, and see in

[1] From Leon Trotsky, *The Revolution Betrayed* (New York: Pathfinder Press Inc., 1970), pp. 86–94. Reprinted by permission of the publisher.

politics a logical argument or a chess match. A political struggle is
in its essence a struggle of interests and forces, not of arguments.
The quality of the leadership is, of course, far from a matter of indifference for the outcome of the conflict, but it is not the only factor,
and in the last analysis is not decisive. Each of the struggling camps
moreover demands leaders in its own image.

The February revolution raised Kerensky and Tseretelli to power,
not because they were "cleverer" or "more astute" than the ruling
tzarist clique, but because they represented, at least temporarily,
the revolutionary masses of the people in their revolt against the
old regime. Kerensky was able to drive Lenin underground and
imprison other Bolshevik leaders, not because the majority of the
workers and soldiers in those days were still following the patriotic
petty bourgeoisie. The personal "superiority" of Kerensky, if it is
suitable to employ such a word in this connection, consisted in the
fact that he did not see farther than the overwhelming majority.
The Bolsheviks in their turn conquered the petty bourgeois democrats, not through the personal superiority of their leaders, but
through a new correlation of social forces. The proletariat had
succeeded at last in leading the discontented peasantry against
the bourgeoisie.

The consecutive stages of the great French Revolution, during its
rise and fall alike, demonstrate no less convincingly that the strength
of the "leaders" and "heroes" that replaced each other consisted
primarily in their correspondence to the character of those classes
and strata which supported them. Only this correspondence, and
not any irrelevant superiorities whatever, permitted each of them
to place the impress of his personality upon a certain historic period.
In the successive supremacy of Mirabeau, Brissot, Robespierre,
Barras and Bonaparte, there is an obedience to objective law incomparably more effective than the special traits of the historic
protagonists themselves.

It is sufficiently well known that every revolution up to this time
has been followed by a reaction, or even a counter-revolution. This,
to be sure, has never thrown the nation all the way back to its
starting point, but it has always taken from the people the lion's
share of their conquests. The victims of the first reactionary wave
have been, as a general rule, those pioneers, initiators, and insti-
gators who stood at the head of the masses in the period of the
revolutionary offensive. In their stead people of the second line, in
league with the former enemies of the revolution, have been ad-

vanced to the front. Beneath this dramatic duel of "coryphées" on the open political scene, shifts have taken place in the relations between classes, and, no less important, profound changes in the psychology of the recently revolutionary masses.

Answering the bewildered questions of many comrades as to what has become of the activity of the Bolshevik party and the working class—where is its revolutionary initiative, its spirit of self-sacrifice and plebeian pride—why, in place of all this, has appeared so much vileness, cowardice, pusillanimity and careerism—Rakovsky referred to the life story of the French revolution of the eighteenth century, and offered the example of Babeuf, who on emerging from the Abbaye prison likewise wondered what had become of the heroic people of the Parisian suburbs. A revolution is a mighty devourer of human energy, both individual and collective. The nerves give way. Consciousness is shaken and characters are worn out. Events unfold too swiftly for the flow of fresh forces to replace the loss. Hunger, unemployment, the death of the revolutionary cadres, the removal of the masses from administration, all this led to such a physical and moral impoverishment of the Parisian suburbs that they required three decades before they were ready for a new insurrection.

The axiom-like assertions of the Soviet literature, to the effect that the laws of bourgeois revolutions are "inapplicable" to a proletarian revolution, have no scientific content whatever. The proletarian character of the October revolution was determined by the world situation and by a special correlation of internal forces. But the classes themselves were formed in the barbarous circumstances of tzarism and backward capitalism, and were anything but made to order for the demands of a socialist revolution. The exact opposite is true. It is for the very reason that a proletariat still backward in many respects achieved in the space of a few months the unprecedented leap from a semifeudal monarchy to a socialist dictatorship, that the reaction in its ranks was inevitable. This reaction has developed in a series of consecutive waves. External conditions and events have vied with each other in nourishing it. Intervention followed intervention. The revolution got no direct help from the west. Instead of the expected prosperity of the country an ominous destitution reigned for long. Moreover, the outstanding representatives of the working class either died in the civil war, or rose a few steps higher and broke away from the masses. And thus after an unexampled tension of forces, hopes and illusions, there came a long period of weariness, decline and sheer disappointment in the results of the revolution. The ebb of the "plebeian pride" made room for a flood of pusillanimity and careerism. The new commanding caste rose to its place upon this wave.

The demobilization of the Red Army of five million played no small role in the formation of the bureaucracy. The victorious commanders assumed leading posts in the local Soviets, in economy, in education, and they persistently introduced everywhere that regime which had ensured success in the civil war. Thus on all sides the masses were pushed away gradually from actual participation in the leadership of the country.

The reaction within the proletariat caused an extraordinary flush of hope and confidence in the petty bourgeois strata of town and country, aroused as they were to new life by the NEP, and growing bolder and bolder. The young bureaucracy, which had arisen at first as an agent of the proletariat, began now to feel itself a court of arbitration between the classes. Its independence increased from month to month.

The international situation was pushing with mighty forces in the same direction. The Soviet bureaucracy became more self-confident, the heavier the blows dealt to the world working class. Between these two facts there was not only a chronological, but a causal connection, and one which worked in two directions. The leaders of the bureaucracy promoted the proletarian defeats; the defeats promoted the rise of the bureaucracy. The crushing of the Bulgarian insurrection and the inglorious retreat of the German workers' party in 1923, the collapse of the Esthonian attempt at insurrection in 1924, the treacherous liquidation of the General Strike in England and the unworthy conduct of the Polish workers' party at the installation of Pilsudski in 1926, the terrible massacre of the Chinese revolution in 1927, and, finally, the still more ominous recent defeats in Germany and Austria—these are the historic catastrophes which killed the faith of the Soviet masses in world revolution, and permitted the bureaucracy to rise higher and higher as the sole light of salvation.

As to the causes of the defeat of the world proletariat during the last thirteen years, the author must refer to his other works, where he has tried to expose the ruinous part played by the leadership in the Kremlin, isolated from the masses and profoundly conservative as it is, in the revolutionary movement of all countries. Here we are concerned primarily with the irrefutable and instructive fact that the continual defeats of the revolution in Europe and Asia, while weakening the international position of the Soviet Union, have vastly strengthened the Soviet bureaucracy. Two dates are especially significant in this historic series. In the second half of 1923, the attention of the Soviet workers was passionately fixed upon Germany, where the proletariat, it seemed, had stretched out its hand to power. The panicky retreat of the German Communist Party was the heaviest possible disappointment to the working masses of the Soviet Union. The Soviet bureaucracy straightway opened a campaign against the theory of "permanent revolution," and dealt the Left Opposition its first cruel blow. During the years 1926 and 1927 the population of the Soviet Union experienced a new tide of hope. All eyes were now directed to the East where the drama of the Chinese revolution was unfolding. The Left Opposition had recovered from the previous blows and was recruiting a phalanx of new adherents. At the end of 1927 the Chinese revolution was massacred by the hangman, Chiang-kai-shek, into whose hands the Communist International had literally betrayed the Chinese workers and peasants. A cold wave of disappointment swept over the masses of the Soviet Union. After an unbridled baiting in the press and at meetings, the bureaucracy finally, in 1928, ventured upon mass arrests among the Left Opposition.

To be sure, tens of thousands of revolutionary fighters gathered around the banner of the Bolshevik-Leninists. The advanced workers were indubitably sympathetic to the Opposition, but that sympathy remained passive. The masses lacked faith that the situation could be seriously changed by a new struggle. Meantime the bureaucracy asserted: "For the sake of an international revolution, the Opposition proposes to drag us into a revolutionary war. Enough of shake-ups! We have earned the right to rest. We will build the socialist society at home. Rely upon us, your leaders!" This gospel of repose firmly consolidated the *apparatchiki* and the military and state officials and indubitably found an echo among the weary workers, and still more the peasant masses. Can it be, they asked themselves, that the Opposition is actually ready to sacrifice the interests of the Soviet Union for the idea of "permanent revolution"? In reality, the struggle had been about the life interests of the Soviet state. The false policy of the International in Germany resulted ten years later in the victory of Hitler—that is, in a threatening war danger from the West. And the no less false policy in China reinforced Japanese imperialism and brought very much nearer the danger in the East. But periods of reaction are characterized above all by a lack of courageous thinking.

The Opposition was isolated. The bureaucracy struck while the iron was hot, exploiting the bewilderment and passivity of the workers, setting their more backward strata against the advanced, and relying more and more boldly upon the kulak and the petty bourgeois ally in general. In the course of a few years, the bureaucracy thus shattered the revolutionary vanguard of the proletariat.

It would be naive to imagine that Stalin, previously unknown to the masses, suddenly issued from the wings full armed with a complete strategical plan. No indeed. Before he felt out his own course, the bureaucracy felt out Stalin himself. He brought it all the necessary guarantees: the prestige of an old Bolshevik, a strong character, narrow vision, and close bonds with the political machine as the sole source of his influence. The success which fell upon him was a surprise at first to Stalin himself. It was the friendly welcome of the new ruling group, trying to free itself from the old principles and from the control of the masses, and having need of a reliable arbiter in its inner affairs. A secondary figure before the masses and in the events of the revolution, Stalin revealed himself as the indubitable leader of the Thermidorian bureaucracy, as first in its midst.

The new ruling caste soon revealed its own ideas, feelings, and, more important, its interests. The overwhelming majority of the older generation of the present bureaucracy had stood on the other side of the barricades during the October revolution. (Take, for example, the Soviet ambassadors only: Troyanovsky, Maisky, Potemkin, Suritz, Khinchuk, etc.) Or at best they had stood aside from the struggle. Those of the present bureaucrats who were in the Bolshevik camp in the October days played in the majority of cases no considerable role. As for the young bureaucrats, they have been chosen and educated by the elders, frequently from among their own offspring. These people could not have achieved the October revolution, but they were perfectly suited to exploit it.

Personal incidents in the interval between these two historic chapters were not, of course, without influence. Thus the sickness and death of Lenin undoubtedly hastened the denouement. Had Lenin lived longer, the pressure of the bureaucratic power would have developed, at least during the first years, more slowly. But as early as 1926 Krupskaya said, in a circle of Left Oppositionists: "If

Ilych were alive, he would probably already be in prison." The fears and alarming prophecies of Lenin himself were then still fresh in her memory, and she cherished no illusions as to his personal omnipotence against opposing historic winds and currents.

The bureaucracy conquered something more than the Left Opposition. It conquered the Bolshevik party. It defeated the program of Lenin, who had seen the chief danger in the conversion of the organs of the state "from servants of society to lords over society." It defeated all these enemies, the Opposition, the party and Lenin, not with ideas and arguments, but with its own social weight. The leaden rump of the bureaucracy outweighed the head of the revolution. That is the secret of the Soviet's Thermidor.

4

The Historian

*Four years of enforced leisure on the Turkish island of Prinkipo resulted in one of Trotsky's masterpieces—*History of the Bolshevik Revolution. *A curiously neglected book (until fairly recently) it provides the reader with a panoramic view of 1917. The following chapter, selected from this three-volume work, shows how Trotsky, who was more inclined to observe and comment on the broad socio-economic forces at work, could deal just as effectively with the immediate implications of the individual in history. For further comment on Trotsky as historian see Bertram Wolfe's evaluation in Chapter 15 of this book.*

THE CZAR AND THE CZARINA[1]

This book will concern itself least of all with those unrelated psychological researches which are now so often substituted for social and historical analysis. Foremost in our field of vision will stand the great, moving forces of history, which are super-personal in character. Monarchy is one of them. But all these forces operate through people. And monarchy is by its very principle bound up with the personal. This in itself justifies an interest in the personality of that monarch whom the process of social development brought face to face with a revolution. Moreover, we hope to show in what follows, partially at least, just where in a personality the strictly personal ends—often much sooner than we think—and how frequently the "distinguishing traits" of a person are merely individual scratches made by a higher law of development.

Nicholas II inherited from his ancestors not only a giant empire, but also a revolution. And they did not bequeath him one quality which would have made him capable of governing an empire or even a province or a county. To that historic flood which was roll-

[1] From Leon Trotsky, *The History of the Russian Revolution*, trans. by Max Eastman (Ann Arbor: University of Michigan Press, 1961), pp. 52–63. Copyright © 1932, 1933, 1960, renewed 1961, by The University of Michigan. Reprinted by permission of the publisher.

ing its billows each one closer to the gates of his palace, the last Romanov opposed only a dumb indifference. It seemed as though between his consciousness and his epoch there stood some transparent but absolutely impenetrable medium.

People surrounding the czar often recalled after the revolution that in the most tragic moments of his reign—at the time of the surrender of Port Arthur and the sinking of the fleet at Tsu-shima, and ten years later at the time of the retreat of the Russian troops from Galicia, and then two years later during the days preceding his abdication when all those around him were depressed, alarmed, shaken—Nicholas alone preserved his tranquillity. He would inquire as usual how many versts he had covered in his journeys about Russia, would recall episodes of hunting expeditions in the past, anecdotes of official meetings, would interest himself generally in the little rubbish of the day's doings, while thunders roared over him and lightnings flashed. "What is this?" asked one of his attendant generals, "a gigantic, almost unbelievable self-restraint, the product of breeding, of a belief in the divine predetermination of events? Or is it inadequate consciousness?" The answer is more than half included in the question. The so-called "breeding" of the czar, his ability to control himself in the most extraordinary circumstances, cannot be explained by a mere external training; its essence was an inner indifference, a poverty of spiritual forces, a weakness of the impulses of the will. That mask of indifference which was called breeding in certain circles, was a natural part of Nicholas at birth.

The czar's diary is the best of all testimony. From day to day and from year to year drags along upon its pages the depressing record of spiritual emptiness. "Walked long and killed two crows. Drank tea by daylight." Promenades on foot, rides in a boat. And then again crows, and again tea. All on the very borderline of physiology. Recollections of church ceremonies are jotted down in the same tone as a drinking party.

In the days preceding the opening of the State Duma, when the whole country was shaking with convulsions, Nicholas wrote: "April 14. Took a walk in a thin shirt and took up paddling again. Had tea in the balcony. Stana dined and took a ride with us. Read." Not a word as to the subject of his reading. Some sentimental English romance? Or a report from the Police Department? "April 15. Accepted Witte's resignation. Marie and Dmitri to dinner. Drove them home to the palace."

On the day of the decision to dissolve the Duma, when the court as well as the liberal circles were going through a paroxysm of fright, the czar wrote in his diary: "July 7. Friday. Very busy morning. Half hour late to breakfast with the officers. . . . A storm came up and it was very muggy. We walked together. Received Goremykin. Signed a decree dissolving the Duma! Dined with Olga and Petia. Read all evening." An exclamation point after the coming dissolution of the Duma is the highest expression of his emotions. The deputies of the dispersed Duma summoned the people to refuse to pay taxes. A series of military uprisings follows: in Sveaborg, Kronstadt, on ships, in army units. The revolutionary terror against high officials was renewed on an unheard-of scale. The czar writes: "July 9. Sunday. It has happened! The Duma was closed to-day. At breakfast after Mass long faces were noticeable among many. . . . The weather was fine. On our walk we met Uncle Misha who came over yesterday from Gatchina. Was quietly busy until dinner and all evening. Went paddling in a canoe." It was in a canoe he went paddling—that is told. But with what he was busy all evening is not indicated. So it was always.

And further in those same fatal days: "July 14. Got dressed and rode a bicycle to the bathing beach and bathed enjoyably in the sea." "July 15. Bathed twice. It was very hot. Only us two at dinner. A storm passed over." "July 19. Bathed in the morning. Received at the farm. Uncle Vladimir and Chagin lunched with us." An insurrection and explosions of dynamite are barely touched upon with a single phrase, "Pretty doings!"—astonishing in its imperturbable indifference, which never rose to conscious cynicism.

"At 9.30 in the morning we rode out to the Caspian regiment . . . walked for a long time. The weather was wonderful. Bathed in the sea. After tea received Lvov and Guchkov." Not a word of the fact that this unexpected reception of the two liberals was brought about by the attempt of Stolypin to include opposition leaders in his ministry. Prince Lvov, the future head of the Provisional Government, said of that reception at the time: "I expected to see the sovereign stricken with grief, but instead of that there came out to meet me a jolly, sprightly fellow in a raspberry-coloured shirt." The czar's outlook was not broader than that of a minor police official—with this difference, that the latter would have a better knowledge of reality and be less burdened with superstitions. The sole paper which Nicholas read for years, and from which he derived his ideas, was a weekly published on state revenue by

Prince Meschersky, a vile, bribed journalist of the reactionary bureaucratic clique, despised even in his own circle. The czar kept his outlook unchanged through two wars and two revolutions. Between his consciousness and events stood always that impenetrable medium—indifference. Nicholas was called, not without foundation, a fatalist. It is only necessary to add that his fatalism was the exact opposite of an active belief in his "star." Nicholas indeed considered himself unlucky. His fatalism was only a form of passive self-defence against historic evolution, and went hand in hand with an arbitrariness, trivial in psychological motivation, but monstrous in its consequences.

"I wish it and therefore it must be——" writes Count Witte. "That motto appeared in all the activities of this weak ruler, who only through weakness did all the things which characterised his reign—a wholesale shedding of more or less innocent blood, for the most part without aim."

Nicholas is sometimes compared with his half-crazy great-great-grandfather Paul, who was strangled by a camarilla acting in agreement with his own son, Alexander "the Blessed." These two Romanovs were actually alike in their distrust of everybody due to a distrust of themselves, their touchiness as of omnipotent nobodies, their feeling of abnegation, their consciousness, as you might say, of being crowned pariahs. But Paul was incomparably more colorful; there was an element of fancy in his rantings, however irresponsible. In his descendant everything was dim; there was not one sharp trait.

Nicholas was not only unstable, but treacherous. Flatterers called him a charmer, bewitcher, because of his gentle way with the courtiers. But the czar reserved his special caresses for just those officials whom he had decided to dismiss. Charmed beyond measure at a reception, the minister would go home and find a letter requesting his resignation. That was a kind of revenge on the czar's part for his own nonentity.

Nicholas recoiled in hostility before everything gifted and significant. He felt at ease only among completely mediocre and brainless people, saintly fakirs, holy men, to whom he did not have to look up. He had his *amour propre*—indeed it was rather keen. But it was not active, not possessed of a grain of initiative, enviously defensive. He selected his ministers on a principle of continual deterioration. Men of brain and character he summoned only in extreme situations when there was no other way out, just as we call

in a surgeon to save our lives. It was so with Witte, and afterwards
with Stolypin. The czar treated both with ill-concealed hostility.
As soon as the crisis had passed, he hastened to part with these
counsellors who were too tall for him. This selection operated so
systematically that the president of the last Duma, Rodzianko, on
the 7th of January, 1917, with the revolution already knocking at
the doors, ventured to say to the czar: "Your Majesty, there is not
one reliable or honest man left around you; all the best men have
been removed or have retired. There remain only those of ill re-
pute."

All the efforts of the liberal bourgeoisie to find a common language with the court came to nothing. The tireless and noisy Rodzianko tried to shake up the czar with his reports, but in vain. The
latter gave no answer either to argument or to impudence, but
quietly made ready to dissolve the Duma. Grand Duke Dmitry, a
former favourite of the czar, and future accomplice in the murder
of Rasputin, complained to his colleague, Prince Yussupov, that the
czar at headquarters was becoming every day more indifferent to
everything around him. In Dmitry's opinion the czar was being fed
some kind of dope which had a benumbing action upon his spiritual
faculties. "Rumours went round," writes the liberal historian Miliukov, "that this condition of mental and moral apathy was sustained
in the czar by an increased use of alcohol." This was all fancy or
exaggeration. The czar had no need of narcotics: the fatal "dope"
was in his blood. Its symptoms merely seemed especially striking on
the background of those great events of war and domestic crisis
which led up to the revolution. Rasputin, who was a psychologist,
said briefly of the czar that he "lacked insides."

This dim, equable and "well-bred" man was cruel—not with the
active cruelty of Ivan the Terrible or of Peter, in the pursuit of
historic aims—What had Nicholas the Second in common with
them?—but with the cowardly cruelty of the late born, frightened
at his own doom. At the very dawn of his reign Nicholas praised the
Phanagoritsy regiment as "fine fellows" for shooting down workers.
He always "read with satisfaction" how they flogged with whips
the bob-haired girl-students, or cracked the heads of defenceless
people during Jewish pogroms. This crowned black sheep gravi-
tated with all his soul to the very dregs of society, the Black Hundred hooligans. He not only paid them generously from the state
treasury, but loved to chat with them about their exploits, and

would pardon them when they accidentally got mixed up in the murder of an opposition deputy. Witte, who stood at the head of the government during the putting down of the first revolution, has written in his memoirs: "When news of the useless cruel antics of the chiefs of these detachments reached the sovereign, they met with his approval, or in any case his defence." In answer to the demand of the governor-general of the Baltic States that he stop a certain lieutenant-captain, Richter, who was "executing on his own authority and without trial non-resistant persons," the czar wrote on the report: "Ah, what a fine fellow!" Such encouragements are innumerable. This "charmer," without will, without aim, without imagination, was more awful than all the tyrants of ancient and modern history.

The czar was mightily under the influence of the czarina, an influence which increased with the years and the difficulties. Together they constituted a kind of unit—and that combination shows already to what an extent the personal, under pressure of circumstances, is supplemented by the group. But first we must speak of the czarina herself.

Maurice Paléologue, the French ambassador at Petrograd during the war, a refined psychologist for French academicians and janitresses, offers a meticulously licked portrait of the last czarina: "Moral restlessness, a chronic sadness, infinite longing, intermittent ups and downs of strength, anguishing thoughts of the invisible other world, superstitions—are not all these traits, so clearly apparent in the personality of the empress, the characteristic traits of the Russian people?" Strange as it may seem, there is in this saccharine lie just a grain of truth. The Russian satirist Saltykov, with some justification, called the ministers and governors from among the Baltic barons "Germans with a Russian soul." It is indubitable that aliens, in no way connected with the people, developed the most pure culture of the "genuine Russian" administrator.

But why did the people repay with such open hatred a czarina who, in the words of Paléologue, had so completely assimilated their soul? The answer is simple. In order to justify her new situation, this German woman adopted with a kind of cold fury all the traditions and nuances of Russian medievalism, the most meagre and crude of all medievalisms, in that very period when the people were making mighty efforts to free themselves from it. This Hessian princess was literally possessed by the demon of autocracy. Having risen from her rural corner to the heights of Byzantine despotism, she would not for anything take a step down. In the orthodox religion she found a mysticism and a magic adapted to her new lot. She believed the more inflexibly in her vocation, the more naked became the foulness of the old regime. With a strong character and a gift for dry and hard exaltations, the czarina supplemented the weak-willed czar, ruling over him.

On March 17, 1916, a year before the revolution, when the tortured country was already writhing in the grip of defeat and ruin, the czarina wrote to her husband at military headquarters: "You must not give indulgences, a responsible ministry, etc. . . . or anything that they want. This must be your war and your peace, and the honour yours and our fatherland's, and not by any means the Duma's. They have not the right to say a single word in these matters." This was at any rate a thoroughgoing programme. And it was in just this way that she always had the whip over the continually vacillating czar.

After Nicholas' departure to the army in the capacity of fictitious commander-in-chief, the czarina began openly to take charge of internal affairs. The ministers came to her with reports as to a regent. She entered into a conspiracy with a small camarilla against the Duma, against the ministers, against the staff-generals, against the whole world—to some extent indeed against the czar. On December 6, 1916, the czarina wrote to the czar: ". . . Once you have said that you want to keep Protopopov, how does he (Premier Trepov) go against you? Bring down your fist on the table. Don't yield. Be the boss. Obey your firm little wife and our Friend. Believe in us." Again three days later: "You know you are right. Carry your head high. Command Trepov to work with him. . . . Strike your fist on the table." Those phrases sound as though they were made up, but they are taken from authentic letters. Besides, you cannot make up things like that.

On December 13 the czarina suggests to the czar: "Anything but this responsible ministry about which everybody has gone crazy. Everything is getting quiet and better, but people want to feel your hand. How long they have been saying to me, for whole years, the same thing: 'Russia loves to feel the whip.' That is *their* nature!" This orthodox Hessian, with a Windsor upbringing and a Byzantine crown on her head, not only "incarnates" the Russian soul, but also organically despises it. *Their* nature demands the whip—writes the Russian czarina to the Russian czar about the Russian people, just two months and a half before the monarchy tips over into the abyss.

In contrast to her force of character, the intellectual force of the czarina is not higher, but rather lower than her husband's. Even more than he, she craves the society of simpletons. The close and long-lasting friendship of the czar and czarina with their lady-in-waiting Vyrubova gives a measure of the spiritual stature of this autocratic pair. Vyrubova has described herself as a fool, and this is not modesty. Witte, to whom one cannot deny an accurate eye, characterised her as "a most common-place, stupid, Petersburg young lady, homely as a bubble in the biscuit dough." In the society of this person, with whom elderly officials, ambassadors and financiers obsequiously flirted, and who had just enough brains not to forget about her own pockets, the czar and czarina would pass many hours, consulting her about affairs, corresponding with her and about her. She was more influential than the State Duma, and even than the ministry.

But Vyrubova herself was only an instrument of "The Friend," whose authority superseded all three. ". . . This is my *private* opinion," writes the czarina to the czar, "I will find out what our Friend thinks." The opinion of the "Friend" is not private, it decides. ". . . I am firm," insists the czarina a few weeks later, "but listen to me, *i.e. this means our Friend,* and trust us in everything. . . . I suffer for you as for a gentle soft-hearted child—who needs guidance, but listens to bad counsellors, while a man sent by God is telling him what he should do."

The Friend sent by God was Gregory Rasputin.

". . . The prayers and the help of our Friend—then all will be well."

"If we did not have Him, all would have been over long ago. I am absolutely convinced of that."

Throughout the whole reign of Nicholas and Alexandra soothsayers and hysterics were imported for the court not only from all over Russia, but from other countries. Special official purveyors arose, who would gather around the momentary oracle, forming a powerful Upper Chamber attached to the monarch. There was no lack of bigoted old women with the title of countess, nor of functionaries weary of doing nothing, nor of financiers who had entire ministries in their hire. With a jealous eye on the unchartered competition of mesmerists and sorcerers, the high priesthood of the Orthodox Church would hasten to pry their way into the holy of holies of the intrigue. Witte called this ruling circle, against which he himself twice stubbed his toe, "the leprous court camarilla."

The more isolated the dynasty became, and the more unsheltered the autocrat felt, the more he needed some help from the other world. Certain savages, in order to bring good weather, wave in the air a shingle on a string. The czar and czarina used shingles for the greatest variety of purposes. In the czar's train there was a whole chapel full of large and small images, and all sort of fetiches, which were brought to bear, first against the Japanese, then against the German artillery.

The level of the court circle really had not changed much from generation to generation. Under Alexander II, called the "Liberator," the grand dukes had sincerely believed in house spirits and witches. Under Alexander III it was no better, only quieter. The "leprous camarilla" had existed always, changing only its personnel and its method. Nicholas II did not create, but inherited from his ancestors, this court atmosphere of savage medievalism. But the country during these same decades had been changing, its problems growing more complex, its culture rising to a higher level. The court circle was thus left far behind.

Although the monarchy did under compulsion make concessions to the new forces, nevertheless inwardly it completely failed to become modernised. On the contrary it withdrew into itself. Its spirit of medievalism thickened under the pressure of hostility and fear, until it acquired the character of a disgusting nightmare overhanging the country.

Towards November 1905—that is, at the most critical moment of the first revolution—the czar writes in his diary: "We got acquainted with a man of God, Gregory, from the Tobolsk province." That was Rasputin—a Siberian peasant with a bald scar on his head, the result of a beating for horse-stealing. Put forward at an appropriate moment, this "Man of God" soon found official helpers—or rather they found him—and thus was formed a new ruling circle which got a firm hold of the czarina, and through her of the czar.

From the winter of 1913–14 it was openly said in Petersburg society that all high appointments, posts and contracts depended upon the Rasputin clique. The "Elder" himself gradually turned into a state institution. He was carefully guarded, and no less carefully sought after by the competing ministers. Spies of the Police Department kept a diary of his life by hours, and did not fail to report how on a visit to his home village of Pokrovsky he got into a drunken and bloody fight with his own father on the street. On the same day that this happened—September 8, 1915—Rasputin sent two friendly telegrams, one to Tsarskoe Selo to the czarina, the other to headquarters to the czar. In epic language the police spies registered from day to day the revels of the Friend. "He returned to-day 5 o'clock in the morning completely drunk." "On the night of the 25–26th the actress V. spent the night with Rasputin." "He arrived with Princess D. (the wife of a gentleman of the bed-chamber of the czar's court) at the Hotel Astoria." . . . And right beside this: "Came home from Tsarskoe Selo about 11 o'clock in the evening." "Rasputin came home with Princess Sh—— very drunk and together they went out immediately." In the morning or evening of the following day a trip to Tsarskoe Selo. To a sympathetic question from the spy as to why the Elder was thoughtful, the answer came: "Can't decide whether to convoke the Duma or not." And then again: "He came home at 5 in the morning pretty drunk." Thus for months and years the melody was played on three keys: "Pretty drunk," "Very drunk," and "Completely drunk." These communications of state importance were brought together and countersigned by the general of gendarmes, Gorbachev.

The bloom of Rasputin's influence lasted six years, the last years of the monarchy. "His life in Petrograd," says Prince Yussupov, who participated to some extent in that life, and afterward killed Rasputin, "became a continual revel, the drunken debauch of a galley slave who had come into an unexpected fortune." "I had at my disposition," wrote the president of the Duma, Rodzianko, "a whole mass of letters from mothers whose daughters had been dishonoured by this insolent rake." Nevertheless the Petrograd metropolitan, Pitirim, owed his position to Rasputin, as also the almost illiterate Archbishop Varnava. The Procuror of the Holy Synod, Sabler, was long sustained by Rasputin; and Premier Kokovtsev was removed at his wish, having refused to receive the "Elder." Rasputin appointed Stürmer President of the Council of Ministers, Protopopov Minister of the Interior, the new Procuror of the Synod, Raev, and many others. The ambassador of the French Republic, Paléologue, sought an interview with Rasputin, embraced him and cried, *"Voilà, un véritable illuminé!"* hoping in this way to win the heart of the czarina to the cause of France. The Jew Simanovich, financial agent of the "Elder," himself under the eye of the Secret Police as a night club gambler and usurer—introduced into the

Ministry of Justice through Rasputin the completely dishonest creature Dobrovolsky.

"Keep by you the little list," writes the czarina to the czar, in regard to new appointments. "Our friend has asked that you talk all this over with Protopopov." Two days later: "Our friend says that Stürmer may remain a few days longer as President of the Council of Ministers." And again: "Protopopov venerates our friend and will be blessed."

On one of those days when the police spies were counting up the number of bottles and women, the czarina grieved in a letter to the czar: "They accuse Rasputin of kissing women, etc. Read the apostles; they kissed everybody as a form of greeting." This reference to the apostles would hardly convince the police spies. In another letter the czarina goes still farther. "During vespers I thought so much about our friend," she writes, "how the Scribes and Pharisees are persecuting Christ pretending that they are so perfect . . . yes, in truth no man is a prophet in his own country."

The comparison of Rasputin and Christ was customary in that circle, and by no means accidental. The alarm of the royal couple before the menacing forces of history was too sharp to be satisfied with an impersonal God and the futile shadow of a Biblical Christ. They needed a second coming of "the Son of Man." In Rasputin the rejected and agonising monarchy found a Christ in its own image.

"If there had been no Rasputin," said Senator Tagantsev, a man of the old regime, "it would have been necessary to invent one." There is a good deal more in these words than their author imagined. If by the word *hooliganism* we understand the extreme expression of those anti-social parasite elements at the bottom of society, we may define Rasputinism as a crowned hooliganism at its very top.

5

The Utopian

In a long and penetrating essay titled Literature and
Revolution, *Trotsky permitted himself an excursion into the
future communist society in order to show what was in store
for mankind. In the style of the great utopian writers of previous centuries, Trotsky presented a picture of the classless society where man is finally able to develop to his fullest capacity
and reach heroic proportions in the process. Perhaps this
idealized vision also helped Trotsky to justify his own great
hardships and sacrifices made for the good life to come.*

THE DREAM [1]

Under Socialism, solidarity will be the basis of society. Literature and art will be tuned to a different key. All the emotions which
we revolutionists, at the present time, feel apprehensive of naming
—so much have they been worn thin by hypocrites and vulgarians—
such as disinterested friendship, love for one's neighbor, sympathy,
will be the mighty ringing chords of Socialist poetry.

However, does not an excess of solidarity, as the Nietzscheans
fear, threaten to degenerate man into a sentimental, passive, herd
animal? Not at all. The powerful force of competition which, in
bourgeois society, has the character of market competition, will not
disappear in a Socialist society, but, to use the language of psychoanalysis, will be sublimated, that is, will assume a higher and more
fertile form. There will be the struggle for one's opinion, for one's
project, for one's taste. In the measure in which political struggles
will be eliminated—and in a society where there will be no classes,
there will be no such struggles—the liberated passions will be
channelized into technique, into construction which also includes
art. Art then will become more general, will mature, will become
tempered, and will become the most perfect method of the progres-

[1] From Leon Trotsky, *Literature and Revolution,* trans. by Rose Strunsky
(Ann Arbor: University of Michigan Press, 1971), pp. 230–31; 253–56. First edi-
tion as an Ann Arbor Paperback 1960. All rights reserved. Reprinted by permission of the publisher.

sive building of life in every field. It will not be merely "pretty" without relation to anything else.

All forms of life, such as the cultivation of land, the planning of human habitations, the building of theaters, the methods of socially educating children, the solution of scientific problems, the creation of new styles, will vitally engross all and everybody. People will divide into "parties" over the question of a new gigantic canal, or the distribution of oases in the Sahara (such a question will exist too), over the regulation of the weather and the climate, over a new theater, over chemical hypotheses, over two competing tendencies in music, and over a best system of sports. Such parties will not be poisoned by the greed of class or caste. All will be equally interested in the success of the whole. The struggle will have a purely ideologic character. It will have no running after profits, it will have nothing mean, no betrayals, no bribery, none of the things that form the soul of "competition" in a society divided into classes. But this will in no way hinder the struggle from being absorbing, dramatic and passionate. And as all problems in a Socialist society —the problems of life which formerly were solved spontaneously and automatically, and the problems of art which were in the custody of special priestly castes—will become the property of all people, one can say with certainty that collective interests and passions and individual competition will have the widest scope and the most unlimited opportunity. Art, therefore, will not suffer the lack of any such explosions of collective, nervous energy, and of such collective psychic impulses which make for the creation of new artistic tendencies and for changes in style. It will be the aesthetic schools around which "parties" will collect, that is, associations of temperaments, of tastes and of moods. In a struggle so disinterested and tense, which will take place in a culture whose foundations are steadily rising, the human personality, with its invaluable basic trait of continual discontent, will grow and become polished at all its points. . . .

The personal dreams of a few enthusiasts today for making life more dramatic and for educating man himself rhythmically, find a proper and real place in this outlook. Having rationalized his economic system, that is, having saturated it with consciousness and planfulness, man will not leave a trace of the present stagnant and worm-eaten domestic life. The care for food and education, which lies like a millstone on the present-day family, will be removed, and will become the subject of social initiative and of an endless collective creativeness. Woman will at last free herself from her semi-servile condition. Side by side with technique, education, in the broad sense of the psycho-physical molding of new generations, will take its place as the crown of social thinking. Powerful "parties" will form themselves around pedagogic systems. Experiments in social education and an emulation of different methods will take place to a degree which has not been dreamed of before. Communist life will not be formed blindly, like coral islands, but will be built consciously, will be tested by thought, will be directed and corrected. Life will cease to be elemental, and for this reason stagnant. Man, who will learn how to move rivers and mountains, how to build peoples' palaces on the peaks of Mont Blanc and at the bottom of the Atlantic, will not only be able to add to his own life richness, brilliancy and intensity, but also a dynamic quality of the highest degree. The shell of life will hardly have time to form before it will burst open again under the pressure of new technical and cultural inventions and achievements. Life in the future will not be monotonous.

More than that. Man at last will begin to harmonize himself in earnest. He will make it his business to achieve beauty by giving the movement of his own limbs the utmost precision, purposefulness and economy in his work, his walk and his play. He will try to master first the semi-conscious and then the subconscious processes in his own organism, such as breathing, the circulation of the blood, digestion, reproduction, and, within necessary limits, he will try to subordinate them to the control of reason and will. Even purely physiologic life will become subject to collective experiments. The human species, the coagulated homo sapiens, will once more enter into a state of radical transformation, and, in his own hands, will become an object of the most complicated methods of artificial selection and psycho-physical training. This is entirely in accord with evolution. Man first drove the dark elements out of industry and ideology, by displacing barbarian routine by scientific technique, and religion by science. Afterwards he drove the unconscious out of politics, by overthrowing monarchy and class with democracy and rationalist parliamentarianism and then with the clear and open Soviet dictatorship. The blind elements have settled most heavily in economic relations, but man is driving them out from there also, by means of the Socialist organization of economic life. This makes it possible to reconstruct fundamentally the traditional family life. Finally, the nature of man himself is hidden in the deepest and darkest corner of the unconscious, of the elemental, of the sub-soil. Is it not self-evident that the greatest efforts of investigative thought and of creative initiative will be in that direction? The human race will not have ceased to crawl on all fours before God, kings and capital, in order later to submit humbly before the dark laws of heredity and a blind sexual selection! Emancipated man will want to attain a greater equilibrium in the work of his organs and a more proportional developing and wearing out of his tissues, in order to reduce the fear of death to a rational reaction of the organism towards danger. There can be no doubt that man's extreme anatomical and physiological disharmony, that is, the extreme disproportion in the growth and wearing out of organs and tissues, give the life instinct the form of a pinched, morbid and hysterical fear of death, which darkens reason and which feeds the stupid and humiliating fantasies about life after death.

Man will make it his purpose to master his own feelings, to raise his instincts to the heights of consciousness, to make them transparent, to extend the wires of his will into hidden recesses, and thereby to raise himself to a new plane, to create a higher social biologic type, or, if you please, a superman.

It is difficult to predict the extent of self-government which the man of the future may reach or the heights to which he may carry his technique. Social construction and psycho-physical self-education will become two aspects of one and the same process. All the arts— literature, drama, painting, music and architecture—will lend this process beautiful form. More correctly, the shell in which the cultural construction and self-education of Communist man will be enclosed, will develop all the vital elements of contemporary art to the highest point. Man will become immeasurably stronger, wiser and subtler; his body will become more harmonized, his movements more rhythmic, his voice more musical. The forms of life will become dynamically dramatic. The average human type will rise to the heights of an Aristotle, a Goethe, or a Marx. And above this ridge new peaks will rise.

PART TWO

THE WORLD LOOKS AT TROTSKY

6

Trotsky as Revolutionary Apprentice

In 1902, the young Trotsky escaped from Siberian exile and left the frontiers of Russia behind him. His initial travels abroad took him through the more important countries of western Europe where, for the first time, he met Lenin and other prominent members of the socialist movement. It was not very long before the French police also became aware of his presence and began to assemble a dossier on his activities. The following brief excerpts from Paris police files draw attention to his strong oratorical powers, which were to captivate crowds of working men and women throughout the greater part of Trotsky's political career.

The second selection is by Alfred Rosmer (born Alfred Griot, 1877–1964), a leading figure in the turn-of-the-century French revolutionary syndicalist movement. Rosmer and Trotsky were attracted to one another because of their implacable opposition to the events of World War I. Orthodox socialist doctrine assumed that the working class would not fight in any future war unleashed by the capitalists. Workers were expected to fight against war either by declaring a general strike or by converting the war into a general class war, which would end in the collapse of capitalism. Events did not support these expectations. By and large, socialist intellectuals and the working class succumbed to national patriotic hysteria and chose to defend their respective countries. The socialists who remained true to the old internationalist ideal were few in number and hopelessly isolated by the upsurge of intense national feeling. Rosmer has left an intimate sketch of Trotsky's life in Paris and of the relentless anti-war activities which eventually led to his expulsion from France.

THE TROTSKY DOSSIER IN THE PARIS POLICE ARCHIVES [1]

October 8, 1903

In Russian circles the rumour persists that the Socialist Party is preparing a grandiose demonstration during the Tsar's visit to Rome.

In order to insult him on Russian territory, the Tsar will be hissed at as he leaves the Russian embassy on his way to the Vatican.

Two members of *Iskra*,[2] Trotsky and Maiser, are being sent from here in order to keep the revolutionary press informed.

Paris, October 12, 1903

Rumours are confirmed that the Tsar will be hissed at in Rome.

Here is a description of Trotsky and Maizer who will go to Rome in order to keep the revolutionary newspapers informed.

Trotsky—between twenty-five and twenty-eight years of age, is five feet three inches tall, has long thick curly brown hair, and a small black mustache. Short-sighted, he wears gold framed glasses. He is talkative, gesticulates much and is very eloquent. He does not speak French very well.

Paris, December 3, 1907

T(rotsky), former chairman of the Petrograd Soviet, held a meeting last night, December 2, in the hall of the Learned Societies on the subject "Capitalism and Socialism." The audience was very large; the meeting began at 9:15 and ended at 11 o'clock.

He spoke about the revolution and similarily about strikes; he described in minute detail the ills and miseries which are a result of general strikes, whether they break out in this country or in neighboring states, but he quickly pointed out that without strikes revolutions would never come to a head.

After having criticized the attitudes of the German Social-Democrats, he began to talk about the raging crisis in America, and then suddenly fainted. The meeting ended.

---

[1] From A. Kriegel, ed. "Le dossier de Trotski a la préfecture de police de Paris", Cahiers du monde russe et soviétique, IV, No. 3 (1963), 276–79; trans. by I. H. Smith.

[2] Iskra (The Spark) was the Russian Social Democrat underground newspaper edited by Plekhanov, Lenin and their collaborators. The first issue appeared December 21, 1900.

Paris, December 7, 1907

Trotsky delivered a lecture last night, December 6, in the building of the Learned Societies on the subject: "The Stages of the Russian Revolution and the Present Political Situation."

Nearly 1000 people were present.

He spoke about the revolution and similarly about strikes; he feat reaction, and to destroy the Tsar's *camarilla* and Nicholas II himself, *it would be necessary to build several dynamite-producing factories.*[4]

He also spoke about the second Duma and Stolypin's[5] attitude, saying that he had crushed the revolution because he had the army on his side.

T(rotsky) concluded that the revolutionists had to conduct active propaganda in the army.

May 19, 1909

A meeting organized by the Russian revolutionists was held last night, May 18, at 190 Choisy Avenue.

There were about 600 persons present.

Trotsky who has not been seen here for a year and a half, spoke about international politics in general, and the Young Turks in particular.

Trotsky is a well known revolutionist who was condemned to exile in Siberia at the time of the conspiracy trial against the Tsar. He is an excellent orator.

TROTSKY IN PARIS DURING WORLD WAR I[6]

Trotsky arrived in Paris alone, some time in the month of November, 1914. He took a room in the Hotel d'Odessa, at the corner of Rue d'Odessa and Boulevard Edgar-Quinet, in the vicinity of the Montparnasse Station. The war had caught him in Vienna where he had immediately become an undesirable enemy alien.

---

[3] The Duma was the first Russian parliamentary government introduced after the Revolution of 1905. The third Duma met in 1907.

[4] This phrase is heavily underlined in red pencil in the original document.

[5] Stolypin, probably the ablest and most determined minister to have served Nicholas II, made a concerted attempt to crush the radical opposition and to implement extensive agricultural reforms. He was assassinated in 1911.

[6] From Alfred Rosmer, "Trotsky in Paris during World War I," in *Leon Trotsky: The Man and His Work* (New York: Merit Publishers, 1969) pp. 103–12. Reprinted by permission of Pathfinder Press.

Viktor Adler[7] had facilitated his departure, and that of his wife and two sons. The family had made its first stop in Zurich, then Trotsky had left to scout out Paris, for that is where he wanted to take up residence. Immediately upon his arrival he went to the editorial office of the paper that the "resisters" [8] were publishing. Its name at the time was *Nashe Slovo* (Our Word) and it was a daily, for the Russian socialists performed the miracle of publishing a socialist daily against the war in wartime Paris, and they published it "to the bitter end," limiting themselves only to changing the name when the French government decided to prohibit it.

One of the first effects of Trotsky's participation in the life of the paper and the group was to place on the order of the day the question of the liaison to establish with the French opposition. He himself was appointed to assure this liaison, along with Martov[9] and a Polish socialist, Lapinski. The three of them were supposed to come to our office and participate in our Tuesday evening meetings. After that I often had occasion to see them, but our subsequent encounters have not weakened the very lively memory I still have of the first evening that found them among us. It was an event. . . .

Let us return to that meeting at which Trotsky, Martov and Lapinski were with us for the first time. As was natural, the conversation remained general at the start, moving from one subject to another. Among our syndicalist friends, some, not many, were still hesitant. The sentimental reaction engendered among them by the aggression of semi-feudal Austria against little Servia, and enhanced by the German thrust through Belgium, disturbed them, and obscured in their minds the true and profound causes of the war. They were to move away from us later on, but they were present that evening, and one of them exclaimed, when the conversation got around more specifically to the war: "But, after all, Austria is the one that jumped cravenly upon Servia!"

Then Trotsky spoke up. The liberal paper of Kiev, *Kievskaya Mysl* (Kievian Thought), with which he had collaborated, had made him a war correspondent during the two Balkan wars. He was thus particularly well equipped for a reply. In the friendly tone that had marked the conversation from the beginning, he gave a

---

[7] Viktor Adler (1852–1918), a physician by training, was the leader of the Austrian Social Democratic Party.

[8] "Resisters" refers to those socialists who actively opposed the war.

[9] Martov (born Y. O. Tsederbaum, 1873–1923), was a close friend of Lenin in the early years, but eventually parted company with the Bolsheviks and became the leader of the Menshevik Party.

luminous exposition of a situation that was complicated only in appearance. The Balkan peoples who had fought against one another were all victims of the diplomatic intrigues and manoeuvers of the Great Powers who regarded them as their pawns on the European chessboard. There was neither smugness nor pedantry in his remarks: an exceptionally well-informed comrade was dealing with a subject which circumstances had enabled him to know thoroughly, in its entirety and in its regional characteristics.

The conclusion forced itself upon us without any need to formulate it, with no room left for doubts and even less for a serious contradiction. All of us had the impression that our group had just gained a remarkable recruit. Our horizon widened. Our meetings were going to take on new life. We felt a great contentment. . . .

No sooner had he arranged himself in wartime Paris—he already knew the city, having made brief visits to it on two occasions, but the state of war had created new complications—than Trotsky hastened to bring in his family. He had found a modest boarding house in the vicinity of Montsouris Park, at the top of La Glacière, at the entrance to Rue de l'Amiral-Mouchez. According to a stubborn but fairly harmless legend—infinitely worse ones were forged—he was always seen at a table of the Café de la Rotonde among the chess players.

There is a mixup here. It is Martov, a bohemian by taste and habit, who was a café frequenter. As for Trotsky, he was the very contrary of a bohemian and he liked neither the atmosphere nor the talk of the café: too much time lost. . . .

The Parisian life of Trotsky was thenceforth well ordered. In the morning, he read the papers. A born journalist, loving, as he reports in his autobiography, to sniff the smell of printer's ink, of freshly moist proofs, he had easily oriented himself among the Parisian press, which was yet so different from what he had been used to in Vienna. . . .

Toward eleven o'clock, he left the house to go to the *Nashe Slovo* printshop, where the editors would come together to discuss and prepare the paper. By their connections with their emigré comrades in Switzerland, England, Scandinavia, America, they were able to gather together, in those days of penury, an exceptional informational service which enabled them to understand better and interpret more exactly the events of each day. The commentaries were accompanied by discussions and important studies that the censor treated with a certain respect, doubtlessly judging that this paper, confined to a small circle of emigrés, represented no danger to the French. In the afternoon and evening, Trotsky wrote, or participated in the debates that the various Russian groups organized. He excelled in enlivening the debates. But he always found the time to occupy himself with the school work of the two boys who, having hardly had the time to start on French, attended a Russian school on the Boulevard Blanqui. . . .

Frightened by the mounting figure of its losses in men, France had decided to appeal to Russia and its "inexhaustible reservoir" to send contingents of Russian soldiers to fight on the French front. The operation was to prove disastrous and shortly after the first disembarkments a grave incident occurred. Russian soldiers stationed in Marseille mutinied; their colonel, unable to mollify them by his eloquence, struck one of them, who turned on him and killed him.

According to the first accounts, the explanation of this tragic affair seemed simple. The Russian soldiers were subject to a severe discipline, they were absolutely forbidden to walk through the city, which was an all the more intolerable regulation when they could see other soldiers of all colors, English, Indian, black, move about freely after their day's military work. Irritation, added to expatriation, was more than enough to explain the fight.

However, disturbing signs appeared. The inquest had disclosed, said the newspapers, that the killer had copies of *Nashe Slovo* in his possession. Thereafter the affair took a different turn: Russian journalists who went into the matter particularly, established the fact that an active role had been played by an agent provocateur. All sorts of documents were then recollected. Gustave Hervé, then still a member of the Administrative Commission of the Socialist Party, had demanded of Minister Malvy, since 1915, to throw out of France all the Russian refugees guilty of revolutionary internationalism. . . . The hour of application had come: on September 15, 1916, the government suppressed *Nashe Slovo*; on September 16 it notified Trotsky of its decree on his expulsion.

The eve of the day set for the expulsion I went to Rue Oudry to greet Trotsky. He received me with a smile: "I am not leaving," he said. Minority socialist deputies had intervened with Briand, then president of the Council, and reminded him that no French government to date had consented to turn over a Russian revolutionist to the czar. Briand denied any such plan; he granted a delay so that a country could be found to admit Trotsky. . . .

If there had been any illusions, they would soon have been dispelled. From that time on, Trotsky was subjected to rigorous police surveillance. Police were installed in an empty shop at the mouth of the Rue Oudry from which no movement of Trotsky could escape their watch. However, Trotsky succeeded one day in outsmarting them. He had been summoned to the police prefecture for noon, and since he could not stand having the police trail him, he left the house before daybreak, resolved to wander around the city throughout the morning. At the stroke of noon, as he approached the office of the commissioner, he had time to perceive the tormented face of the policeman, upset at having let him escape. Shortly after this interlude, the order for his immediate expulsion arrived, this time definitively. That day, when I appeared at Rue Oudry, I found only Natalia and the two boys, who were preparing to leave for Spain; two new police agents, more important ones, had presented themselves that morning. . . .

7
Trotsky in Revolution
and Civil War

The following extracts, taken from the period of the Revolution and the Civil War, present a picture of Trotsky in the heat of battle. The first is from the diary of N. H. Sukhanov, a member of the Menshevik party, who had the peculiar knack of being in the right place at the right time. He graphically describes how Trotsky, a member of the Petrograd Soviet, saved Victor Chernov's life from a frenzied crowd.

The second is taken from John Reed's celebrated book Ten Days that Shook the World. *Though it depicts Trotsky in a curiously comic situation, it says perhaps a great deal more about the level of political awareness among the Russian masses in this period.*

The extract by Alexander Barmine portrays Trotsky at the height of his career, as chief of the Red Army. Barmine, who was a young cadet officer, attended a lecture delivered by Trotsky.

The extracts by Angelica Balabanoff, a woman who devoted most of her life to the socialist cause, and Louise Bryant, an American journalist, reveal the rigidly puritanical life style of Trotsky in his first years in power.

SUKHANOV OBSERVES TROTSKY IN ACTION [1]

I went to the meeting-hall.[2] From the windows of the crowded corridor looking on to the square I saw an endless multitude packing the entire space as far as the eye could reach. Armed men were climbing through the open windows. A mass of placards and banners with the Bolshevik slogans (of June 9th) rose above the crowd. As

[1] From N. Sukhanov (Himmer), *The Russian Revolution, 1917: A Personal Record*, tr., ed., and abridged by Joel Carmichael (London: Oxford University Press, 1955), pp. 444–47. Reprinted by permission of the publisher.

[2] The meeting-hall was the Taurida Palace, built by Catherine the Great. In 1906 the Palace first served as the seat of the Imperial Duma. In 1917 the Palace housed both the Provisional Government and the Petrograd Soviet.

before in the left corner of the square the black, ugly masses of armoured cars loomed up.

I forced my way into the ante-chamber, which was completely packed; lines and groups of people, in the midst of the noise and clanking of arms, for some reason or other were excitedly pushing back and forth. Suddenly someone tugged at my sleeve; Lesha Emelyanova, an old SR[3] friend recently back from prison and now on the staff of Izvestiya, stood before me. She was pale and trembling violently.

"Go quickly—Chernov's[4] been arrested—the Kronstadters[5]—here in the courtyard! Quickly, quickly . . . They may kill him!"

I rushed towards the doors. Just then I saw Raskolnikov pushing his way towards the Catherine Hall. I seized him by the arm and pulled him back with me, explaining on the way what the trouble was: if Raskolnikov couldn't pacify the Kronstadters, who could? But it wasn't easy to get out: there was a crush in the porch. Raskolnikov followed me obediently, but answered me ambiguously. I was perplexed and began to lose my temper. We had already pushed through to the steps when Trotsky, shouldering aside the crowd, overtook us. He was also hurrying to Chernov's rescue.

It seemed that this was what had happened. When the Central Ex. Com. was told that the Kronstadters were demanding the Socialist Ministers, the Praesidium sent Chernov out to them. No sooner had he appeared at the top of the steps of the entry-way than the Kronstadters became very aggressive; shouts arose from the armed crowd of many thousands: "Search him! See whether he's armed!"

"In that case I won't speak," Chernov declared, and started back into the Palace.

Then the crowd got relatively calm. Chernov made a short speech

---

[3] The Social Revolutionary Party, simply referred to as the S.R., was essentially the peasant party of Russia. It also had the largest mass following in Russia during the Revolutionary period.

[4] Victor M. Chernov (1873–1952) was the leader of the S.R.'s and served as Minister of Agriculture in the Provisional Government. The crowd surrounding the Taurida Palace was demanding that the Soviets assume full power and dismiss the Provisional Government. The masses in the streets felt that the Provisional Government no longer reflected their interests. One inflamed activist in the crowd waved his fist in Chernov's face and shouted, "Take the power, you son of a bitch, when they offer it to you!"

[5] Kronstadt was the great Tsarist naval base close to Petrograd on the Baltic. During the Revolution the Bolsheviks secured considerable support from the sailors referred to here as the Kronstadters.

about the Government crisis, sharply condemning the Cadets who had left the Government. The speech was interrupted by shouts of a Bolshevik character. And towards the end some enterprising person in the crowd demanded that the Socialist Ministers at once declare the land national property, etc.

There arose a frantic din. The crowd, brandishing its weapons, began to surge forward. A group of people tried to get Chernov inside the Palace, but strong hands seized him and put him in an open car standing close to the steps at the right of the porch. Chernov was declared under arrest as a hostage.

A group of workers immediately rushed off to report all this to the Central Ex. Com.; bursting into the White Hall they produced a panic by shouting out: "Comrade Chernov has been arrested by the mob! They're tearing him to pieces right now! To the rescue! Everyone out into the street!"

Chkheidze,[6] restoring order with difficulty, proposed that Kamenev, Martov, Lunacharsky,[7] and Trotsky should hasten to rescue Chernov. I don't know where the others were, but Trotsky got there in time.

Raskolnikov and I had stopped on the top step near the right side of the porch—when Trotsky, two steps below us, climbed up on the bonnet of a car. The mob was in turmoil as far as the eye could reach. Around the motor-car a number of sailors with rather savage faces were particularly violent. Chernov, who had plainly lost all presence of mind, was in the back seat.

All Kronstadt knew Trotsky and, one would have thought, trusted him. But he began to speak and the crowd did not subside. If a shot had been fired nearby at that moment by way of provocation, a tremendous slaughter might have occurred, and all of us, including perhaps Trotsky, might have been torn to shreds. Trotsky, excited and not finding words in this savage atmosphere, could barely make the nearest rows listen to him. But what was he saying?

"You hurried over here, Red Kronstadters, as soon as you heard the revolution was in danger! Red Kronstadt has once again shown itself to be the champion of the proletarian cause. Long live Red Kronstadt, the glory and pride of the revolution! . . ."

Nevertheless he was listened to with hostility. When he tried to

---

[6] Nicholas S. Chkheidze (1864–1926) was a prominent member of the Menshevik Party.

[7] Kamenev (born Leo Rosenfeld, 1883–1936) and Anatole V. Lunacharsky (1875–1933) were members of the Bolshevik Party.

pass on to Chernov himself, the ranks around the car again began raging.

"You've come to declare your will and show the Soviet that the working class no longer wants to see the bourgeoisie in power. But why hurt your own cause by petty acts of violence against casual individuals? Individuals are not worthy of your attention . . . Every one of you has demonstrated his devotion to the revolution. Every one of you is ready to lay down his life for it. I know that. Give me your hand, Comrade! Your hand, brother!"

Trotsky stretched his hand down to a sailor who was protesting with especial violence. But the latter firmly refused to respond, and moved his hand—the one which was not holding a rifle—out of reach. If these were people alien to the revolution or outright provocateurs, to them Trotsky was just as bad as Chernov, or much worse: they might be waiting only for an opportunity to settle accounts with both advocate and defendant. But I think they were Kronstadt naval ratings who had, in their own judgement, accepted Bolshevik ideas. It seemed to me that the sailor, who must have heard Trotsky in Kronstadt more than once, now had a real feeling that he was a traitor: he remembered his previous speeches and was confused. Let Chernov go? Then why had he been summoned?

Not knowing what to do, the Kronstadters released Chernov. Trotsky took him by the arm and hurried him off into the Palace.

JOHN REED VISITS BOLSHEVIK HEADQUARTERS [8]

I spent a great deal of time at Smolny.[9] It was no longer easy to get in. Double rows of sentries guarded the outer gates, and once inside the front door there was a long line of people waiting to be let in, four at a time, to be questioned as to their identity and their business. Passes were given out, and the pass system was changed every few hours; for spies continually sneaked through. . . .

One day as I came up to the outer gate I saw Trotsky and his wife just ahead of me. They were halted by a soldier. Trotsky searched through his pockets, but could find no pass.

"Never mind," he said finally. "You know me. My name is Trotsky."

[8] From John Reed, *Ten Days that Shook the World* (New York: Random House, 1935), pp. 48–50. Footnotes Copyright © 1960 by Random House, Inc. Reprinted by permission of Random House, Inc.

[9] The Smolny Institute, situated in Petrograd, was originally a school for young ladies, and then became Bolshevik headquarters in 1917.

"You haven't got a pass," answered the soldier stubbornly. "You cannot go in. Names don't mean anything to me."

"But I am the president of the Petrograd Soviet."

"Well," replied the soldier, "if you're as important a fellow as that you must at least have one little paper."

Trotsky was very patient. "Let me see the Commandant," he said. The soldier hesitated, grumbling something about not wanting to disturb the Commandant for every devil that came along. He beckoned finally to the soldier in command of the guard. Trotsky explained matters to him. "My name is Trotsky," he repeated.

"Trotsky?" The other soldier scratched his head. "I've heard the name somewhere," he said at length. "I guess it's all right. You can go in, comrade. . . ."

CADET OFFICER BARMINE ATTENDS A LECTURE GIVEN BY TROTSKY [10]

Trotsky was very different from Lenin, and in some respects complemented him. Where Lenin was informal and genial, Trotsky was formal and a little aloof. I remember when he first addressed us at the Staff College. The meeting had been announced for eight o'clock, and generally, in the traditional Russian fashion, a meeting so announced would start at nine or ten. Trotsky, however, ascended the platform exactly as the clock was striking the hour. That was his custom, and it had a strong effect upon the minds of us Russians. His entrance was imposing, in spite of his plain uniform, devoid of insignia. His pointed beard, flashing eyes, and broad shoulders gave an impression of angular force which, when he spoke, was emphasized by his sharp gestures and metallic voice.

Unlike Lenin, who rarely resorted to passionate diatribes, Trotsky hurled a fiery flow of invective against Churchill, Poincaré, and the other imperialists who were trying to strangle the Revolution by blockade. His bitter irony and assurance carried us with him. But as soon as he had finished he left the hall. There was no personal contact in the corridors. This aloofness, I believe, may partly explain Trotsky's inability as well as his unwillingness to build a large personal following among the rank and file of the Party. Against the intrigues of Party leaders, which were soon to multiply,

[10] From Alexander Barmine, *One Who Survived* (New York: G. P. Putnam's Sons, 1945), pp. 93–94. Copyright © 1945 by Alexander Barmine. Reprinted by permission of the publisher.

Trotsky fought only with the weapons he knew how to use: his pen and his oratory. And even these weapons he took up only when it was too late. With his proud passivity and quixotism it was easy for the unscrupulous and relentless Stalin, a master of intrigue, to outmaneuver Trotsky.

THE REVOLUTIONARY LEADER IN PRIVATE LIFE

Angelica Balabanoff [11]

Men are usually judged not according to their qualities or defects but rather on the basis of what makes the contact with them pleasant or difficult, and the opinions about Trotsky were often onesided and unjust. Very few, for example, knew of his self-inflicted privations. Had he been willing to avail himself of the privileges to which his position entitled him, he and his family could have lived in much better circumstances. He was misjudged by those who turned to him with petitions or pleas, the validity and urgency of which he understood without being able to satisfy them. Because of his omnipotent air and his militaristic tone, which colored even his personal relations, it never occurred to those who came to him for help that he might not be able to grant it.

One day a woman came to see me who had offered hospitality to Trotsky when he, under tsarism, had been sought by the police. Now she came to beseech him for help: her pharmacy, the family's only source of income, was to be expropriated. She wanted to see him and ask his intervention in her favor. I knew he would be able to do nothing for her, it being a case of law enforcement. To claim exceptional treatment, to make one's influence or power felt, did not occur to any of us who fought with such determination the nepotism of the preceding governments.

Knowing from experience what it means to have to deny when, inside us, is the urge to grant, to mitigate suffering, I wanted to spare Trotsky this torture and went to see him about this matter myself. He confirmed my assumption: his intercession was impossible. In our talk we recalled the sad cases of those in whose behalf we should have liked to intervene and the anguish we had felt at not being able to do so. "Just think," Trotsky said to me, "for two

[11] From Angelica Balabanoff, *Impressions of Lenin* (Ann Arbor: University of Michigan Press, 1964), pp. 132–35. Copyright © 1964 by The University of Michigan. Trans. Isotta Cesari. Reprinted by permission of the publisher.

years now my father has been wanting to see me, but he has no
shoes and I cannot get them for him. With so many people around
who are without shoes, how could I request shoes for my father?"

With regard to himself he did not act differently. He ate inade-
quately, although he suffered from a stomach disorder. If he was
able to endure the burden and strain of his demanding position, it
was due, in part, to the fact that during his travels he ate with the
general staff. For him, the observance of every Soviet ordinance
was a matter of principle, a question of honor. He was the first to
observe the discipline he taught others, and his private conduct was
never in contradiction with his position as the leader of a revolutionary army. In the most dangerous and difficult moments, in immediate proximity of the enemy, he would march at the head of
the army although he had been advised, in the interest of the republic, not to risk his life.

In October 1919 the war between White and Red Russia had
come to a turning point: White Russia seemed to have won. 25,000
men, well armed, well fed, and headed by the notorious General
Kornilov, were at the gates of Petrograd. The defenders, ill clad,
ill fed, disorganized, and discouraged, would not be able—it seemed
—to resist. The signs of inevitable defeat were everywhere.

Lenin, more deeply aware than the others of the meaning of
irreparable defeat the loss of the Red capital held, asked of Trotsky
what no ruler under similar circumstances could have demanded of
a military leader. In Siberia and eastern Russia the attacks of a
well-equipped army under Kolchak's command had to be sustained; Denikin had established himself in Central Russia, and the
British army was supplied with everything necessary to defeat a
much stronger and better-equipped enemy than the Red Army was
at that time.

But Lenin's order was: "Petrograd must be defended to the last
drop of blood! Every street, every house in it must be defended, if
necessary!" As always, Trotsky gave himself body and soul to the
reorganization and the moral preparation of the troops at his dis-
posal for the defense of Petrograd. As he went on in his arduous
task it became evident that the sparse ranks of his army needed re-
plenishing. Mobilization and more mobilization! To that end the
young communists called a meeting in Moscow. Trotsky, Alexandra
Kollontai, and I were to speak.

When the situation at the gates of Petrograd had become extremely grave and every effort to save the city seemed doomed,

Trotsky decided to head the troops himself and to lead them to a duel of unequal arms. This decision, however, he kept to himself. That evening death was not mentioned, although it was before everyone's eyes—the effect of Trotsky's powerful rhetoric, the sense of tragedy created by his words. That evening he did not stamp out his words: he spoke solemnly, without affectation. It seemed to me that if death had entered the hall that very moment to choose his victims, every man in that immense crowd would have been vying for the honor. Never before or since did I hear Trotsky speak as on that evening.

Before it came to Lenin's mind that Trotsky would be the man—the only one, in fact—who could bring Russia to such a state of preparedness as to be able to defend herself, he had treated him with unveiled hostility. But as soon as it occurred to Lenin to make use of him in the interest of Bolshevism, he appointed him to the highest office and changed his public and private attitude toward him. At that time Trotsky was for him the irreplaceable Bolshevik, unequaled in his tireless, manifold activity and his boundless devotion to the cause. . . .

Louise Bryant[12]

During the first days of the Bolshevik revolt I used to go every morning to Smolny to get the latest news. Trotsky and his pretty little wife, who hardly ever spoke anything but French, lived in one room on the top floor. The room was partitioned off like a poor artist's attic studio. In one end were two cots and a cheap little dresser and in the other a desk and two or three cheap wooden chairs. There were no pictures, no comfort anywhere. Trotsky occupied this office all the time he was Minister of Foreign Affairs and many dignitaries found it necessary to call upon him there.

Outside the door two Red Guards kept constant watch. They looked rather menacing, but were really friendly. It was always possible to get an audience with Trotsky.

Running a government was a new task and often puzzling to the people in Smolny. They had a certain awe of Lenine, so they left him pretty well alone, while every little difficulty under the sun was brought to Trotsky. He worked hard and was often on the verge of a nervous breakdown; he became irritable and flew into

[12] From Louise Bryant, *Six Red Months in Russia* (New York: G. H. Doran Co., 1918), pp. 145–46.

rages. For a long time he refused to use a stenographer and labori-ously wrote out all his letters by hand. A few months of experience, however, made him change his methods. He got two efficient stenographers and the Red Guards were replaced by aides who had once been officers in the regular army.

Trotsky is slight of build, wears thick glasses and has dark, stormy eyes. His forehead is high and his hair black and wavy. He is a brilliant and fiery orator. After knowing him the stories about German money seem utterly absurd. He steadfastly refused to take money from his father, in exile he was desperately poor. Both Lenine and Trotsky live with great frugality. Both receive, at their own request, but fifty dollars a month as the highest officials of the Russian government. I think a psychoanalyst would say of Trotsky that he has a "complex" about money. He was so afraid of plots to implicate him that he threw people out of his office when they came to offer honest and legitimate financial aid to Russia. . . .

8
Trotsky Appraised by the Early Bolsheviks

*Exposed to the fierce and scalding anti-Trotsky prop-
aganda poured out by Soviet authorities over the decades, we
find it difficult to imagine that Trotsky's contributions to the
making of the Revolution and the winning of the Civil War
were ever reported in print in Soviet Russia.*

*Here are excerpts from two important Bolshevik writers of
the early twenties who had personal contact with Trotsky
over a considerable period of time and were in a position to
judge his abilities. The first selection is by Karl Radek (1885–
1939), a revolutionist of Polish origin, who played an active role
in the Communist International, and was regarded as the most
capable of Bolshevik journalists. The article, unashamedly
flattering in tone, appeared as a major piece in* Pravda.

*The second selection is by Anatoly V. Lunacharsky (1873–
1933), who served as the first commissar of education in the
Soviet government under Lenin. As an objective attempt to
evaluate Trotsky the man, it is of much greater value than
Radek's essay because it was written at a moment, as E. H.
Carr has explained, "when it was already possible to criticize
Trotsky and not yet obligatory to abuse him."*

KARL RADEK [1]

History has prepared our party for various tasks. However
defective our state machinery or our economic activity may be, still
the whole past of the party has psychologically prepared it for the
work of creating a new order of economy and a new state apparatus.
History has even prepared us for diplomacy. It is scarcely necessary
to mention that world politics have always occupied the minds of
Marxists. But it was the endless negotiations with the Mensheviki
that perfected our diplomatic technique; and it was during these

[1] From *Pravda,* March 14, 1923.

69

old struggles that Comrade Chicherin[2] learned to draw up diplomatic notes. We are just beginning to learn the miracle of economics. Our state machinery creaks and groans. In one thing, however, we have been eminently successful—in our Red Army. Its creator, its central will, is Comrade L. D. Trotsky.

Old General Moltke, the creator of the German army, often spoke of the danger that the pen of the diplomats might spoil the work of the soldier's sabre. Warriors the world over, though there were classical authors among them, have always opposed the pen to the sword. The history of the proletarian revolution shows how the pen may be re-forged into a sword. Trotsky is one of the best writers of world socialism, but these literary advantages did not prevent him from becoming the leader, the leading organizer of the first proletarian army. The pen of the best publicist of the revolution was re-forged into a sword.

The literature of scientific socialism helped Comrade Trotsky but little in solving the problems which confronted the party when it was threatened by world imperialism. If we look through the whole of pre-war socialist literature, we find—with the exception of a few little-known works by Engels, some chapters in his Anti-Duehring devoted to the development of strategy, and some chapters in Mehring's excellent book on Lessing, devoted to the war activity of Frederick the Great. . . .

I do not know to what extent Comrade Trotsky occupied himself before the war with questions of military knowledge. I believe that he did not gain his gifted insight into these questions from books, but received his impetus in this direction at the time when he was acting as correspondent in the Balkan war, this final rehearsal of the great war. It is probable that he deepened his knowledge of war technique and of the mechanism of the army, during his sojourn in France (during the war), from where he sent his brilliant war sketches to the *Kiev Mysli*. It may be seen from this work how magnificently he grasped the spirit of the army. The Marxist Trotsky saw not only the external discipline of the army, the cannon, the technique. He saw the living human beings who serve the instruments of war, he saw the sprawling charge on the field of battle.

Trotsky is the author of the first pamphlet giving a detailed analysis of the causes of the decay of the International. Even in face of

[2] Gregory Chicherin was Soviet Commissar of Foreign Affairs at that time (1923).

this great decay Trotsky did not lose his faith in the future of socialism; on the contrary, he was profoundly convinced that all those qualities which the bourgeoisie endeavors to cultivate in the uniformed proletariat, for the purpose of securing its own victory, would soon turn against the bourgeoisie, and serve not only as the foundation of the revolution, but also of revolutionary armies. One of the most remarkable documents of his comprehension of the class structure of the army, and of the spirit of the army, is the speech which he made—I believe at the first Soviet Congress and in the Petrograd Workers' and Soldiers' Council—on Kerensky's July offensive.[3] In this speech Trotsky predicted the collapse of the offensive, not only on technical military grounds, but on the basis of the political analysis of the condition of the army.

"You"—and here he addressed himself to the Mensheviki and the SR's—"demand from the government a revision of the aims of the war. In doing so you tell the army that the old aims, in whose name Czarism and the bourgeoisie demanded unheard-of sacrifices, did not correspond to the interests of the Russian peasantry and Russian proletariat. You have not attained a revision of the aims of the war. You have created nothing to replace the Czar and the fatherland, and yet you demand of the army that it shed its blood for this nothing. We cannot fight for nothing, and your adventure will end in collapse."

The secret of Trotsky's greatness as organizer of the Red Army lies in this attitude of his towards the question.

All great military writers emphasize the tremendously decisive significance of the moral factor in war. One half of Clausewitz's[4] great book is devoted to this question, and the whole of our victory in the civil war is due to the circumstance that Trotsky knew how to apply this knowledge of the significance of the moral factor in war to our reality. When the old Czarist army went to pieces, the minister of war of the Kerensky government, Verkhovsky, proposed that the older military classes be discharged, the military authorities behind the front partly reduced, and the army reorganized by the introduction of fresh young elements. When we seized power, and

---

[3] Kerensky, who eventually became Prime Minister in the Provisional Government, was convinced that only a military victory against the Germans and Austrians would guarantee the survival of the Government. In July he launched an offensive against the Austrians which quickly resulted in catastrophe for the Russian Army.

[4] Karl Von Clausewitz (1780–1831), a Prussian military officer, was the first of modern writers to make a complete study of all aspects of warfare.

the trenches emptied, many of us made the same proposition. But this idea was the purest Utopia. It was impossible to replace the fleeing Czarist army with fresh forces. These two waves would have crossed and divided each other. The old army had to be completely dissolved; the new army could only be built up on the alarm sent out by Soviet Russia to the workers and peasants, to defend the conquests of the revolution.

When, in April 1918, the best Czarist officers who remained in the army after our victory met together for the purpose of working out, in conjunction with our comrades and some military representatives of the Allies, the plan of organization for the army, Trotsky listened to their plans for several days—I have a clear recollection of this scene—in silence. These were the plans of people who did not comprehend the upheaval going on before their eyes. Every one of them replied to the question of how an army was to be organized on the old pattern. They did not grasp the metamorphosis wrought in the human material upon which the army is based. How the war experts laughed at the first voluntary troops organized by Comrade Trotsky in his capacity as Commissar of War! Old Borisov, one of the best Russian military writers, assured those Communists with whom he was obliged to come in contact, time and again, that nothing would come of this undertaking, that the army could only be built up on the basis of general conscription, and maintained by iron discipline. He did not grasp that the volunteer troops were the secure foundation pillars upon which the structure was to be erected, and that the masses of peasants and workers could not possibly be rallied around the flag of war again unless the broad masses were confronted by deadly danger. Without believing for a single moment that the volunteer army could save Russia, Trotsky organized it as an apparatus which he required for the creation of a new army.

But Trotsky's organizing genius, and his boldness of thought are even more clearly expressed in his courageous determination to utilize the war specialists for creating the army. Every good Marxist is fully aware that in building up a good economic apparatus we still require the aid of the old capitalist organization. Lenin defended this proposition with the utmost decision in his April speech on the tasks of the Soviet power. In the mature circles of the party the idea is not contested. But the idea that we could create an instrument for the defense of the republic, an army, with the aid of the Czarist officers—encountered obstinate resistance. Who could think of re-arming the White officers who had just been disarmed? Thus many comrades questioned. I remember a discussion on this question among the editors of the *Communist*, the organ of the so-called left communists, in which the question of the employment of staff officers nearly led to a split. And the editors of this paper were among the best schooled theoreticians and practicians of the party. It suffices to mention the names of Bukharin, Ossonski, Lomov, W. Yakovlev. There was even greater distrust among the broad circles of our military comrades, recruited for our military organizations during the war. The mistrust of our military functionaries could only be allayed, their agreement to the utilization of the knowledge possessed by the old officers could only be won, by the burning faith of Trotsky in our social force, the belief that we could obtain from the war experts the benefit of their science, without permitting them to force their politics upon us; the belief that the revolutionary watchfulness of the progressive workers would enable them to overcome any counter-revolutionary attempts made by the staff officers.

In order to emerge victorious, it was necessary for the army to be headed by a man of iron will, and for this man to possess not only the full confidence of the party, but the ability of subjugating with his iron will the enemy who is forced to serve us. But Comrade Trotsky has not only succeeded in subordinating to his energy even the highest staff officers. He attained more: he succeeded in winning the confidence of the best elements among the war experts, and in converting them from enemies of Soviet Russia to its most profoundly convinced followers. I witnessed one such victory of Trotsky's at the time of the Brest-Litovsk negotiations.[5] The officers who had accompanied us to Brest-Litovsk maintained a more than reserved attitude towards us. They fulfilled their role as experts with the utmost condescension, in the opinion that they were attending a comedy which merely served to cover a business transaction long since arranged between the Bolsheviki and the German government. But the manner in which Trotsky conducted the struggle against German imperialism, in the name of the principles of the Russian revolution, forced every human being present in the assembly room to feel the moral and spiritual victory of this eminent representative

[5] Brest-Litovsk refers to the Treaty signed on March 3, 1918 which ended the war for Soviet Russia.

of the Russian proletariat. The mistrust of the war experts towards us vanished in proportion to the development of the great Brest-Litovsk drama.

How clearly I recollect the night when Admiral Altvater—who has since died—one of the leading officers of the old regime, who began to help Soviet Russia not from motives of fear but of conscience, entered my room and said: "I came here because you forced me to do so. I did not believe you; but now I shall help you, and do my work as never before, in the profound conviction that I am serving the fatherland." It is one of Trotsky's greatest victories that he has been able to impart the conviction that the Soviet government really fights for the welfare of the Russian people, even to such people who have come over to us from hostile camps on compulsion only. It goes without saying that this great victory on the inner front, this moral victory over the enemy, has been the result not only of Trotsky's iron energy which won for him universal respect; not only the result of the deep moral force, the high degree of authority even in military spheres, which this socialist writer and people's tribune, who was placed by the will of the revolution at the head of the army, has been able to win for himself; this victory has also required the self-denial of tens of thousands of our comrades in the army, an iron discipline in our own ranks, a consistent striving towards our aims; it has also required the miracle that those masses of human beings who only yesterday fled from the battle-field, take up arms again today, under much more difficult conditions, for the defense of the country.

That these politico-psychological mass factors played an important role is an undeniable fact, but the strongest, most concentrated, and striking expression of this influence is to be found in the personality of Trotsky. Here the Russian revolution has acted through the brain, the nervous system, and the heart of its greatest representative. When our first armed trial began, with Czecho-Slovakia, the party, and with it its leader Trotsky, showed how the principle of the political campaign—as already taught by Lassalle[6]—could be applied to war, to the fight with "steel arguments." We concentrated all material and moral forces on the war. The whole party had grasped the necessity of this. But this necessity also finds its highest expression in the steel figure of Trotsky. After our victory

---

[6] Ferdinand Lassalle (1825–1864) was a prominent Germany labor organizer and acquaintance of Karl Marx.

over Denikin[7] in March 1920, Trotsky said, at the party conference: "We have ravaged the whole of Russia in order to conquer the Whites." In these words we again find the unparalleled concentration of will required to ensure the victory. We needed a man who was the embodiment of the war-cry, a man who became the tocsin sounding the alarm, the will demanding from one and all an unqualified subordination to the great bloody necessity.

It was only a man who works like Trotsky, a man who spares himself as little as Trotsky, who can speak to the soldiers as only Trotsky can—it was only such a man who could be the standard bearer of the armed working people. He has been everything in one person. He has thought out the strategic advice given by the experts and has combined it with a correct estimate of the proportions of social forces; he knew how to unite in one movement the impulses of fourteen fronts, of the ten thousand communists who informed headquarters as to what the real army is and how it is possible to operate with it; he understood how to combine all this in one strategic plan and one scheme of organization. And in all this splendid work he understood better than anyone else how to apply the knowledge of the significance of the moral factor in war.

This combination of strategist and military organizer with the politician is best characterized by the fact that during the whole of this hard work, Trotsky appreciated the importance of Demian Bedny (communist writer), or of the artist Moor (who draws most of the political caricatures for the communist papers, posters, etc.) for the war. Our army was an army of peasants, and the dictatorship of the proletariat with regard to the army, that is, the leading of this peasants' army by workers and by representatives of the working class, was realized in the personality of Trotsky and in the comrades cooperating with him. Trotsky was able, with the aid of the whole apparatus of our party, to impart to the peasants' army, exhausted by the war, the profoundest conviction that it was fighting in its own interests.

Trotsky worked with the whole party in the work of forming the Red Army. He would not have fulfilled his task without the party. But without him the creation of the Red Army and its victories, would have demanded infinitely greater sacrifices. Our party will go down in history as the first proletarian party which suc-

---

[7] General Anton I. Denikin (1872–1947) was one of several White generals who crossed swords with Trotsky.

ceeded in creating a great army, and this bright page in the history
of the Russian revolution will always be bound up with the name
of Leon Davidovitch Trotsky, with the name of a man whose work
and deeds will claim not only the love, but also the scientific study
of the young generation of workers preparing to conquer the whole
world.

ANATOLY V. LUNACHARSKY [8]

Trotsky entered the history of our Party somewhat unexpect-
edly and with instant brilliance. As I have heard, he began his
social-democratic activity on the school bench and he was exiled
before he was eighteen.

He escaped from exile. He first caused comment when he appeared
at the Second Party Congress, at which the split occurred. Trotsky
evidently surprised people abroad by his eloquence, by his education, which was remarkable for a young man, and by his aplomb.
An anecdote was told about him which is probably not true, but
which is nevertheless characteristic, according to which Vera Ivanovna Zasulich, with her usual expansiveness, having met Trotsky,
exclaimed in the presence of Plekhanov: 'That young man is undoubtedly a genius'; the story goes that as Plekhanov left the meeting he said to someone: 'I shall never forgive this of Trotsky.' It is
a fact that Plekhanov did not love Trotsky, although I believe that
it was not because the good Zasulich called him a genius but because Trotsky had attacked him during the 2nd Congress with
unusual heat and in fairly uncomplimentary terms. Plekhanov at
the time regarded himself as a figure of absolutely inviolable majesty in social-democratic circles; even outsiders who disagreed with
him approached him with heads bared and such cheekiness on
Trotsky's part was bound to infuriate him. The Trotsky of those
days undoubtedly had a great deal of juvenile bumptiousness. If
the truth be told, because of his youth nobody took him very seriously, but everybody admitted that he possessed remarkable talent
as an orator and they sensed too, of course, that this was no chick
but a young eagle.

I first met him at a comparatively late stage, in 1905, after the

[8] From Anatoly V. Lunacharsky, *Revolutionary Silhouettes*, trans. from the
Russian and ed. by Michael Glenny (New York: Hill and Wang Inc., 1967), pp.
59–69. Copyright © 1967 by Anatoly Vasilievich Lunacharsky. Translation
Copyright © 1967 by Michael Glenny. Reprinted by permission of Hill and
Wang, a division of Farrar, Straus & Giroux, Inc., and Penguin Books Ltd.

events of January.[9] He had arrived, I forget where from, in Geneva and he and I were due to speak at a big meeting summoned as a result of this catastrophe. Trotsky then was unusually elegant, unlike the rest of us, and very handsome. This elegance and his nonchalant, condescending manner of talking to people, no matter who they were, gave me an unpleasant shock. I regarded this young dandy with extreme dislike as he crossed his legs and pencilled some notes for the impromptu speech that he was to make at the meeting. But Trotsky spoke very well indeed.

He also spoke at an international meeting, where I spoke for the first time in French and he in German; we both found foreign languages something of an obstacle, but we somehow survived the ordeal. Then, I remember, we were nominated—I by the Bolsheviks, he by the Mensheviks—to some commission on the division of joint funds and there Trotsky adopted a distinctly curt and arrogant tone.

Until we returned to Russia after the first (1905) revolution I did not see him again, nor did I see much of him during the course of the 1905 revolution. He held himself apart not only from us but from the Mensheviks too. His work was largely carried out in the Soviet of Workers' Deputies and together with Parvus[10] he organized some kind of a separate group which published a very militant, very well-edited small and cheap newspaper.[11]

I remember someone saying in Lenin's presence: 'Khrustalev's star is waning and now the strong man in the Soviet is Trotsky.' Lenin's face darkened for a moment, then he said: 'Well, Trotsky has earned it by his brilliant and unflagging work.'

Of all the Mensheviks Trotsky was then the closest to us, but I do not remember him once taking part in the fairly lengthy discussions between us and the Mensheviks on the subject of reuniting. By the Stockholm congress[12] he had already been arrested.

[9] The events of January refer to 'Bloody Sunday' (9 January 1905) when a peaceful workers' procession, headed by the priest Father Gapon, marched through Petersburg to present a petition to the Tsar and was shot down by troops.

[10] Dr. Alexander L. Helphand, alias Parvus (1867–1924). Of Russo-German origin, simultaneously a brilliant revolutionary schemer and a businessman, Parvus was the go-between who channelled German government funds to the Bolsheviks with the aim of disrupting Russia's war effort.

[11] This newspaper, called *Nachalo* (The Beginning) replaced *Iskra* (The Spark) as the party journal. It began publication on 10 November 1905 in St Petersburg. Besides Trotsky and Parvus, Dan and Martov also contributed to it.

[12] The 4th Congress of the Russian Social Democratic party, held in April 1906. Called the 'Unification' Congress, as it temporarily healed the breach

His popularity among the Petersburg proletariat at the time of his arrest was tremendous and increased still more as a result of his picturesque and heroic behaviour in court. I must say that of all the social-democratic leaders of 1905–6 Trotsky undoubtedly showed himself, despite his youth, to be the best prepared. Less than any of them did he bear the stamp of a certain kind of émigré narrowness of outlook which, as I have said, even affected Lenin at that time. Trotsky understood better than all the others what it meant to conduct the political struggle on a broad, national scale. He emerged from the revolution having acquired an enormous degree of popularity, whereas neither Lenin nor Martov had effectively gained any at all. Plekhanov had lost a great deal, thanks to his display of quasi-Kadet[13] tendencies. Trotsky stood then in the very front rank. . . .

I must say here and now that Trotsky was extremely bad at organizing not only the Party but even a small group of it. He had practically no whole-hearted supporters at all; if he succeeded in impressing himself on the Party, it was entirely by his personality. The fact that he was quite incapable of fitting into the ranks of the Mensheviks made them react to him as though he were a kind of social-democratic anarchist and his behaviour annoyed them greatly. There was no question, at that time, of his total identification with the Bolsheviks. Trotsky seemed to be closest to the Martovites and indeed he always acted as though he were.

His colossal arrogance and an inability or unwillingness to show any human kindness or to be attentive to people, the absence of that charm which always surrounded Lenin, condemned Trotsky to a certain loneliness. One only has to recall that even a number of his personal friends (I am speaking, of course, of the political sphere) turned into his sworn enemies; this happened, for instance, in the case of his chief lieutenant, Semkovsky,[14] and it occurred later with the man who was virtually his favourite disciple, Skobeliev.[15]

---

between the Bolsheviks and the Mensheviks and re-admitted the 'Bund' to the party.

[13] 'Kadet,' from the Russian initial letters of the words 'Constitutional Democrats,' was the name of the left-wing liberal political party founded in 1905. The party dominated the first Duma in 1906 and in subsequent Dumas formed the chief opposition party. The party and particularly its leader Milyukov played a major part in the Provisional Government. The Kadets were outlawed by the Bolsheviks at their seizure of power in October–November 1917.

[14] Semyon Yulievich Bronstein, alias Semkovsky (1882–?). Journalist. A Menshevik until 1920, then joined the Bolshevik party.

[15] Matvey Ivanovich Skobeliev (1885–1939). Joined the Social Democratic party

Trotsky had little talent for working within political bodies; however, in the great ocean of political events, where such personal traits were completely unimportant, Trotsky's entirely positive gifts came to the fore. . . .

I have always regarded Trotsky as a great man. Who, indeed, can doubt it? In Paris he had grown greatly in stature in my eyes as a statesman and in the future he grew even more. I do not know whether it was because I knew him better and he was better able to demonstrate the full measure of his powers when working on a grander scale or because in fact the experience of the revolution and its problems really did mature him and enlarge the sweep of his wings.

The agitational work of spring 1917 does not fall within the scope of these memoirs but I should say that under the influence of his tremendous activity and blinding success certain people close to Trotsky were even inclined to see in him the real leader of the Russian revolution. Thus for instance the late M. S. Uritsky,[16] whose attitude to Trotsky was one of great respect, once said to me and I think to Manuilsky:[17] 'Now that the great revolution has come one feels that however intelligent Lenin may be he begins to fade beside the genius of Trotsky.' This estimation seemed to me incorrect, not because it exaggerated Trotsky's gifts and his force of character but because the extent of Lenin's political genius was then still not obvious. Yet it is true that during that period, after the thunderous success of his arrival in Russia and before the July days, Lenin did keep rather in the background, not speaking often, not writing much, but largely engaged in directing organizational work in the Bolshevik camp, whilst Trotsky thundered forth at meetings in Petrograd.

Trotsky's most obvious gifts were his talents as an orator and as a writer. I regard Trotsky as probably the greatest orator of our age. In my time I have heard all the greatest parliamentarians and popular tribunes of socialism and very many famous orators of the

---

in 1903, worked as an agitator in Baku. Menshevik deputy to the Fourth Duma, 1912. Minister of Labour in the Provisional Government. Emigrated in 1920. Returned to U.S.S.R. 1922. Liquidated in the thirties purge.

[16] Moisei Solomonovich Uritsky (1873–1918).

[17] Dmitri Zakharevich Manuilsky (1883–1959). Became a Social Democrat 1903. Belonged (with Lunacharsky) to the left-wing 'Forward' group and the 'Inter-district' group. Joined the Bolsheviks 1917. Central Committee of the Ukrainian C.P. since 1920. Ukrainian delegate to the U.N. and 'foreign minister' of the Ukraine 1944–52.

bourgeois world and I would find it difficult to name any of them, except Jaurès[18] (Bebel [19] I only heard when he was an old man), whom I could put in the same class as Trotsky.

His impressive appearance, his handsome, sweeping gestures, the powerful rhythm of his speech, his loud but never fatiguing voice, the remarkable coherence and literary skill of his phrasing, the richness of imagery, scalding irony, his soaring pathos, his rigid logic, clear as polished steel—those are Trotsky's virtues as a speaker. He can speak in lapidary phrases, or throw off a few unusually well-aimed shafts and he can give a magnificent set-piece political speech of the kind that previously I had only heard from Jaurès. I have seen Trotsky speaking for two and a half to three hours in front of a totally silent, standing audience listening as though spellbound to his monumental political treatise. Most of what Trotsky had to say I knew already and naturally every politician often has to repeat the same ideas again and again in front of new crowds, yet every time Trotsky managed to clothe the same thought in a different form. I do not know whether Trotsky made so many speeches when he became War Minister of our great republic during the revolution and civil war: it is most probable that his organizational work and tireless journeying from end to end of the vast front left him little time for oratory, but even then Trotsky was above all a great political agitator. His articles and books are, as it were, frozen speech —he was literary in his oratory and an orator in literature.

It is thus obvious why Trotsky was also an outstanding publicist, although of course it frequently happened that the spell-binding quality of his actual speech was somewhat lost in his writing.

As regards his inner qualities as a leader Trotsky, as I have said, was clumsy and ill-suited to the small-scale work of Party organization. This defect was to be glaringly evident in the future, since it was above all the work in the illegal underground of such men as Lenin, Chernov and Martov which later enabled their parties to contend for hegemony in Russia and later, perhaps, all over the world. Trotsky was hampered by the very definite limitations of his own personality.

[18] Jean Auguste Jaurès (1899–1914). Professor of philosophy, Toulouse University. French Socialist Party leader. Founder and first editor of L'Humanité. Assassinated at the outbreak of the First World War for his anti-militarist views.

[19] August Bebel (1830–1913). Early German socialist. Chairman of the S.P.D. Prominent in the Second International.

Trotsky as a man is prickly and overbearing. However, after Trotsky's merger with the Bolsheviks, it was only in his attitude to Lenin that Trotsky always showed—and continues to show—a tactful pliancy which is touching. With the modesty of all truly great men he acknowledges Lenin's primacy.

On the other hand as a man of political counsel Trotsky's gifts are equal to his rhetorical powers. It could hardly be otherwise, since however skilful an orator may be, if his speech is not illuminated by thought he is no more than a sterile virtuoso and all his oratory is as a tinkling cymbal. It may not be quite so necessary for an orator to be inspired by love, as the apostle Paul maintains, for he may be filled with hate, but it is essential for him to be a thinker. Only a great politician can be a great orator, and since Trotsky is chiefly a political orator, his speeches are naturally the expression of political thinking.

It seems to me that Trotsky is incomparably more orthodox than Lenin, although many people may find this strange. Trotsky's political career has been somewhat tortuous: he was neither a Menshevik nor a Bolshevik but sought the middle way before merging his brook in the Bolshevik river, and yet in fact Trotsky has always been guided by the precise rules of revolutionary Marxism. Lenin is both masterful and creative in the realm of political thought and has very often formulated entirely new lines of policy which subsequently proved highly effective in achieving results. Trotsky is not remarkable for such boldness of thought: he takes revolutionary Marxism and draws from it the conclusions applicable to a given situation. He is as bold as can be in opposing liberalism and semi-socialism, but he is no innovator.

At the same time Lenin is much more of an opportunist, in the profoundest sense of the word. This may again sound odd—was not Trotsky once associated with the Mensheviks, those notorious opportunists? But the Mensheviks' opportunism was simply the political flabbiness of a petty-bourgeois party. I am not referring to this sort of opportunism; I am referring to that sense of reality which leads one now and then to alter one's tactics, to that tremendous sensitivity to the demands of the time which prompts Lenin at one moment to sharpen both edges of his sword, at another to place it in its sheath.

Trotsky has less of this ability; his path to revolution has followed a straight line. These differing characteristics showed up in the famous clash between the two leaders of the great Russian revolution over the peace of Brest-Litovsk.[20]

It is usual to say of Trotsky that he is ambitious. This, of course, is utter nonsense. I remember Trotsky making a very significant remark in connection with Chernov's acceptance of a ministerial portfolio: 'What despicable ambition—to abandon one's place in history in exchange for the untimely offer of a ministerial post.' In that, I think, lay all of Trotsky. There is not a drop of vanity in him, he is totally indifferent to any title or to the trappings of power; he is, however, boundlessly jealous of his own role in history and in that sense he is ambitious. Here he is I think as sincere as he is in his natural love of power.

Lenin is not in the least ambitious either. I do not believe that Lenin ever steps back and looks at himself, never even thinks what posterity will say about him—he simply gets on with his job. He does it through the exercise of power, not because he finds power sweet but because he is convinced of the rightness of what he is doing and cannot bear that anyone should harm his cause. His ambitiousness stems from his colossal certainty of the rectitude of his principles and too, perhaps, from an inability (a very useful trait in a politician) to see things from his opponent's point of view. Lenin never regards an argument as a mere discussion; for him an argument is always a struggle, which under certain circumstances may develop into a fight. Lenin always welcomes the transition from a struggle to a fight.

In contrast to Lenin, Trotsky is undoubtedly often prone to step back and watch himself. Trotsky treasures his historical role and would probably be ready to make any personal sacrifice, not excluding the greatest sacrifice of all—that of his life—in order to go down in human memory surrounded by the aureole of a genuine revolutionary leader. His ambition has the same characteristic as that of Lenin, with the difference that he is more often liable to make mistakes, lacking as he does Lenin's almost infallible instinct, and being a man of choleric temperament he is liable, although only temporarily, to be blinded by passion, whilst Lenin, always on

---

[20] Lenin, aware of the total collapse of the Russian army in 1918 and of the consequences of a German seizure of Petrograd, demanded peace at any price; Trotsky, chief Bolshevik negotiator with the Germans at Brest-Litovsk, refused to sign the Treaty and proclaimed a state of 'neither peace nor war,' i.e. a unilateral armistice declared by Russia and withdrawal of Russian troops. Lenin won, after furious debate in the Party Central Committee, and Sokolnikov and Chicherin signed the harsh peace terms on behalf of Russia.

an even keel and always in command of himself, is virtually incapable of being distracted by irritation.

It would be wrong to imagine, however, that the second great leader of the Russian revolution is inferior to his colleague in everything; there are, for instance, aspects in which Trotsky incontestably surpasses him—he is more brilliant, he is clearer, he is more active. Lenin is fitted as no one else to take the chair at the Council of Peoples' Commissars and to guide the world revolution with the touch of genius, but he could never have coped with the titanic mission[21] which Trotsky took upon his own shoulders, with those lightning moves from place to place, those astounding speeches, those fanfares of on-the-spot orders, that role of being the unceasing electrifier of a weakening army, now at one spot, now at another. There is not a man on earth who could have replaced Trotsky in that respect.

Whenever a truly great revolution occurs, a great people will always find the right actor to play every part and one of the signs of greatness in our revolution is the fact that the Communist Party has produced from its own ranks or has borrowed from other parties and incorporated into its own organism sufficient outstanding personalities who were suited as no others to fulfil whatever political function was called for.

And two of the strongest of the strong, totally identified with their roles, are Lenin and Trotsky.

[21] Titanic Mission refers to Trotsky's appointment as Commissar for War (1918–1922), when he virtually created the Red Army and beat the combined Allied and "White" Russian forces.

9

Trotsky Observed from Afar

*The following extracts were written by contempo-
raries of Trotsky who had never met him in person, but
nevertheless followed his career with deep interest. The first
essay, by Sir Winston Churchill, is perhaps the most vitriolic
attack on Trotsky to appear in print with the possible exception of the storm of abuse poured out by Soviet writers. One
will find neither balance nor objectivity in this sketch, but
rather a wild, almost hysterical denunciation of Trotsky, who
so skillfully thwarted British strategic plans and interests in
both war-time and post-war Russia. The sketch reveals a good
deal more about Churchill's elemental abhorrence of communism than it sheds illumination on the mystery of Trotsky's
personality. However, it remains a fascinating commentary on
Tory opinion.*

*The second selection is an early (1918) and little-known
essay by Sir Lewis Namier, one of England's outstanding historians. Although Namier's greatest contribution was made in
the field of eighteenth-century English political studies, he
maintained an interest in East European affairs. A conservative
in politics and outlook, Namier was able to go much further
than Churchill in recognizing the complexities of Trotsky's
role in Russian history.*

SIR WINSTON CHURCHILL[1]

When the usurper and tyrant is reduced to literary controversy,
when the Communist instead of bombs produces effusions for the
capitalist Press, when the refugee War Lord fights his battles over
again, and the discharged executioner becomes chatty and garrulous
at his fireside, we may rejoice in the signs that better days are come.
I have before me an article that Leon Trotsky alias Bronstein has
recently contributed to *John o' London's Weekly* in which he deals

[1] From Winston S. Churchill, *Great Contemporaries* (New York: G. P. Putnam's Sons, 1937), pp. 167–68; 170–74. Reprinted by permission of The Hamlyn
Publishing Group Limited.

with my descriptions of Lenin, with the Allied Intervention in Russia, with Lord Birkenhead and other suggestive topics. He has written this article from his exile in Turkey while supplicating England, France and Germany to admit him to the civilizations it has been—and still is—the object of his life to destroy. Russia—his own Red Russia—the Russia he had framed and fashioned to his heart's desire regardless of suffering, all his daring, all his writing, all his harangues, all his atrocities, all his achievements, have led only to this—that another 'comrade,' his subordinate in revolutionary rank, his inferior in wit, though not perhaps in crime, rules in his stead, while he, the once triumphant Trotsky whose frown meted death to thousands, sits disconsolate—a skin of malice stranded for a time on the shores of the Black Sea and now washed up in the Gulf of Mexico.

But he must have been a difficult man to please. He did not like the Czar, so he murdered him and his family. He did not like the Imperial Government, so he blew it up. He did not like the liberalism of Guchkov[2] and Miliukov,[3] so he overthrew them. He could not endure the Social Revolutionary moderation of Kerensky[4] and Savinkov,[5] so he seized their places. And when at last the Communist regime for which he had striven with might and main was established throughout the whole of Russia, when the Dictatorship of the Proletariat was supreme, when the New Order of Society had passed from visions into reality, when the hateful culture and traditions of the individualist period had been eradicated, when the Secret Police had become the servants of the Third International, when in a word his Utopia had been achieved, he was still discontented. He still fumed, growled, snarled, bit and plotted. He had raised the poor against the rich. He had raised the penniless against the poor. He had raised the criminal against the penniless. All had fallen out as he had willed. But nevertheless the vices of human society required, it seemed, new scourgings. In the deepest depth he sought with desperate energy for a deeper. But—poor

[2] Alexander Guchkov (1862–1936), contrary to Churchill's evaluation, was not a liberal but a wealthy conservative Moscow industrialist who led the Octoberist Party, perhaps the most conservative party in Russia.

[3] Paul Miliukov (1859–1943), a historian by training, was the leader of the Constitutional Democrats, or Cadet party.

[4] Alexander Kerensky (1881–1970), a moderate socialist, served as Minister of Justice and eventually became Premier of the Provisional Government before the Bolsheviks took power in October.

[5] Boris Savinkov (1879–1925), radical novelist and former terrorist, served in the Provisional Government and fought against the Bolsheviks.

wretch—he had reached rock-bottom. Nothing lower than the Communist criminal class could be found. In vain he turned his gaze upon the wild beasts. The apes could not appreciate his eloquence. He could not mobilize the wolves, whose numbers had so notably increased during his administration. So the criminals he had installed stood together, and put him outside.

Hence these chatty newspaper articles. Hence these ululations from the Bosphorus. Hence these entreaties to be allowed to visit the British Museum and study its documents, or to drink the waters of Malvern for his rheumatism, or of Nauheim for his heart, or of Homburg for his gout, or of some other place for some other complaint. Hence these broodings in Turkish shades pierced by the searching eye of Mustafa Kemal. Hence these exits from France, from Scandinavia. Hence this last refuge in Mexico.

It is astonishing that a man of Trotsky's intelligence should not be able to understand the well-marked dislike of civilized governments for the leading exponents of Communism. He writes as if it were due to mere narrow-minded prejudice against new ideas and rival political theories. But Communism is not only a creed. It is a plan of campaign. . . .

It is probable that Trotsky never comprehended the Marxian creed: but of its drill-book he was the incomparable master. He possessed in his nature all the qualities requisite for the art of civic destruction—the organizing command of a Carnot, the cold detached intelligence of a Machiavelli, the mob oratory of a Cleon, the ferocity of Jack the Ripper, the toughness of Titus Oates. No trace of compassion, no sense of human kinship, no apprehension of the spiritual, weakened his high and tireless capacity for action. Like the cancer bacillus he grew, he fed, he tortured, he slew in fulfillment of his nature. He found a wife who shared the Communist faith. She worked and plotted at his side. She shared his first exile to Siberia in the days of the Czar. She bore him children. She aided his escape. He deserted her. He found another kindred mind in a girl of good family who had been expelled from a school at Kharkov for persuading the pupils to refuse to attend prayers and to read Communist literature instead of the Bible. By her he had another family. As one of his biographers (Max Eastman) puts it: 'If you have a perfectly legal mind, she is not Trotsky's wife, for Trotsky never divorced Alexandra Ivovna Sokolovski, who still uses the name of Bronstein.' Of his mother he writes in cold and chilling terms. His father—old Bronstein—died of typhus in 1920 at the age of 83. The triumphs of his son brought no comfort to this honest hard-working and believing Jew. Persecuted by the Reds because he was a bourgeois; by the Whites because he was Trotsky's father, and deserted by his son, he was left to sink or swim in the Russian deluge, and swam on steadfastly to the end. What else was there for him to do?

Yet in Trotsky, in this being so removed from the ordinary affections and sentiments of human nature, so uplifted, shall we say, above the common herd, so superbly fitted to his task, there was an element of weakness especially serious from the Communist point of view. Trotsky was ambitious, and ambitious in quite a common worldly way. All the collectivism in the world could not rid him of an egoism which amounted to a disease, and to a fatal disease. He must not only ruin the State, he must rule the ruins thereafter. Every system of government of which he was not the head or almost the head was odious to him. The Dictatorship of the Proletariat to him meant that he was to be obeyed without question. He was to do the dictating on behalf of the proletariat. 'The toiling masses,' the 'Councils of Workmen, Peasants and Soldiers,' the gospel and revelation of Karl Marx, the Federal Union of Socialist Soviet Republics, etc., to him were all spelt in one word: Trotsky. This led to trouble. Comrades became jealous. They became suspicious. At the head of the Russian Army, which he reconstructed amid indescribable difficulties and perils, Trotsky stood very near the vacant throne of the Romanovs.

The Communist formulas he had used with devastating effect upon others, were now no impediment to him. He discarded them as readily as he had discarded his wife, or his father, or his name. The Army must be remade; victory must be won; and Trotsky must do it and Trotsky profit from it. To what other purpose should revolutions be made? He used his exceptional prowess to the full. The officers and soldiers of the new model army were fed, clothed and treated better than anyone else in Russia. Officers of the old Czarist regime were wheedled back in thousands. 'To the devil with politics—let us save Russia.' The salute was reintroduced. The badges of rank and privilege were restored. The authority of commanders was re-established. The higher command found themselves treated by this Communist upstart with a deference they had never experienced from the Ministers of the Czar. The abandonment by the Allies of the Russian Loyalist cause crowned these measures with a victory easy but complete. In 1922 so great was the appreciation among the military for Trotsky's personal attitude and system that he might well have been made Dictator of Russia by the armed forces, but for one fatal obstacle.

He was a Jew. He was still a Jew. Nothing could get over that. Hard fortune when you have deserted your family, repudiated your race, spat upon the religion of your fathers, and lapped Jew and Gentile in a common malignity, to be baulked of so great a prize for so narrow-minded a reason! Such intolerance, such pettiness, such bigotry were hard indeed to bear. And this disaster carried in its train a greater. In the wake of disappointment loomed catastrophe.

For meanwhile the comrades had not been idle. They too had heard the talk of the officers. They too saw the possibilities of a Russian Army reconstituted from its old elements. While Lenin lived the danger seemed remote. Lenin indeed regarded Trotsky as his political heir. He sought to protect him. But in 1924 Lenin died: and Trotsky, still busy with his army, still enjoying the day-to-day work of administering his department, still hailed with the acclamations which had last resounded for Nicholas II, turned to find a hard and toughly-wrought opposition organized against him.

Stalin, the Georgian, was a kind of General Secretary to the governing instrument. He managed the caucus and manipulated the innumerable committees. He gathered the wires together with patience and pulled them in accordance with a clearly-perceived design. When Trotsky advanced hopefully, confidently indeed, to accept the succession to Lenin, the party machine was found to be working in a different direction. In the purely political arena of Communist activities Trotsky was speedily outmaneuvered. He was accused on the strength of some of his voluminous writings of 'Anti-Leninism.' He does not seem to have understood that Lenin had replaced God in the Communist mind. He remained for some time under the impression that any such desirable substitution had been effected by Trotsky. He admitted his heresy and eagerly explained to the soldiers and workers the very cogent reasons which had led him to it. His declarations were received with blank dismay. The OGPU [6] was set in motion. Officers known to be under an obligation to Trotsky were removed from their appointments. After a period of silent tension he was advised to take a holiday. This holiday after some interruptions still continues.

[6] OGPU, or Unified State Political Administration, was the secret police organization which replaced the original Cheka.

Stalin used his success to build a greater. The Politbureau, without the spell of Lenin, or the force of Trotsky, was in its turn purged of its remaining elements of strength. The politicians who had made the Revolution were dismissed and chastened and reduced to impotence by the party manager. The caucus swallowed the Cabinet, and with Stalin at its head became the present Government of Russia. Trotsky was marooned by the very mutineers he had led so hardily to seize the ship.

What will be his place in history? For all its horrors, a glittering light plays over the scenes and actors of the French Revolution. The careers and personalities of Robespierre, of Danton, even of Marat, gleam luridly across a century. But the dull, squalid figures of the Russian Bolsheviks are not redeemed in interest even by the magnitude of their crimes. All form and emphasis is lost in a vast process of Asiatic liquefaction. Even the slaughter of millions and the misery of scores of millions will not attract future generations to their uncouth lineaments and outlandish names. And now most of them have paid the penalty of their crimes. They have emerged from the prison-cells of the Cheka, to make their strange unnatural confessions to the world. They have met the death in secret to which they had consigned so many better and braver men.

But Trotsky survives. He lingers on the stage. He has forgotten his efforts, which Lenin restrained, to continue the War against Germany rather than submit to the conditions of Brest-Litovsk. He has forgotten his own career as a War Lord and the opportunist remaker of the Russian Army. In misfortune he has returned to Bolshevik Orthodoxy. Once again he has become the exponent of the purest sect of Communism. Around his name gather the new extremists and doctrinaires of world-revolution. Upon him is turned the full blast of Soviet malignity. The same vile propaganda which he used with so much ruthlessness upon the old Regime, is now concentrated upon himself by his sole-surviving former comrade. All Russia from Poland to China, from the North Pole to the Himalayas, is taught to regard him as the supreme miscreant seeking in some way or other to add new chains to the workers, and bring the Nazi invader into their midst. The name of Lenin, the doctrine of Karl Marx, are invoked against him at the moment when he frantically endeavors to exploit them. Russia is regaining strength as the virulence of Communism abates in her blood. The process may be cruel, but it is not morbid. It is a need of self-preservation which impels the Soviet Government to extrude Trotsky and his fresh-distilled poisons. In vain he screams his protests against a hurricane of lies; in vain he denounces the bureaucratic tyranny of which he would so blithely be the head; in vain he strives to rally the underworld of Europe to the overthrow of the Russian Army he was once proud to animate. Russia has done with him, and done with him forever.

He will perhaps have leisure to contemplate his handiwork. No one could wish him a better punishment than that his life should be prolonged, and that his keen intelligence and restless spirit should corrode each other in impotence and stultification. Indeed we may foresee a day when his theories, exploded by their application, will have ceased even to be irritating to the active, hopeful world outside, and when the wide tolerance which follows from a sense of security, will allow him to creep back, discredited and extinct, to the European and American haunts, where so many of his early years were spent. It may be that in these future years, he will find as little comfort in the work which he has done, as his father found in the son he had begotten.

SIR LEWIS NAMIER [7]

When a student of the Juridical Faculty at Odessa, Trotsky joined the Socialist movement. Some revolutionary fracas or conspiracy led to his expulsion from the University and started him on his career of Socialist propaganda, diversified by years in Siberia and in prison. The men of the Russian Revolution are now frequently described in Western Europe as "wind-bags" or "talkers" by people who have never known Russian prisons or Siberia. Let them read the gruesome story of Maria Spiridonova,[8] which at one time made the whole civilised world shudder (the recent Peasants' Congress at Petrograd elected Maria Spiridonova its president). Or let them read Leo Deutsch's "Reminiscences of Siberia," or any other lives from that new martyrology. There has been horror in the past experience of these men and women: a madness has been engendered by it and a fanaticism which alone has enabled them to endure all things and conquer in the end.

In Trotsky the fanatic is much less conspicuous than in most

---

[7] Sir Lewis Namier, "Trotsky." From *The New Europe* (London: January 1918). Reprinted by permission of Lady Julia Namier.

[8] Maria Spiridonova (1889–?), a former terrorist, eventually became the leader of an extreme faction of the social revolutionaries known as the left S.R.'s.

Bolshevik leaders. Socialism supplies him with an outlook rather than with doctrines. He is clear-sighted, he understands the logic of events, the force of ideas, their uncompromising nature, and the need for simplicity and cogency in political thinking. Where minor men are unbending from pedantry, experience forbids Trotsky to compromise in matters of principle. He knows the only terms on which one can fight with the arms of the spirit against material weapons, and he knows how to capture the man behind the machine gun, instead of countering the two in their own kind. In 1905 he fought autocracy and succumbed—the Russian army had remained with the Tsar: twelve years later it went over to the Revolution. In July 1917 he fought Kerensky and succumbed: the army was with his rival. In November he won without having raised or armed new forces. He is now (January 1918) trying the same game on Germany, nay, on the entire world—each man has only one method of acting, just as he has only one face.

Can Trotsky win this time? He will undoubtedly succumb again, but the seed will have been sown. That quaint idea of "the dictatorship of the proletariat" will remain, a burning sign to those who have a sense of wrong: it is not democracy which the Bolsheviks aim at, but "a turn of the wheel"—the rule of the downtrodden. They address to the upper classes what Meredith calls "the parent question of humanity: 'Am I thy master or thou mine?' " If their sign is to endure, if their teachings are to work in the consciousness of the masses, they must remain pure. For ideas, compromise with reality means a kind of decay; it may be like the decay of fruit at seedtime; but if the fruit perishes when the seed is still immature, the loss is unredeemed and uncompensated. Conservatism is the philosophy of reality; revolution results from the logic of ideas.

If Trotsky compromises, he is lost; if he does not, he is probably lost too—which few men are likely to regret more than he himself. He is not a calm, iron ascetic with a deeply human heart and an inhuman mind, like Lenin. His *naturel* has proved too strong even for the long schooling of Russian revolutionary life. Trotsky enjoys life, loves pleasure, is very ambitious and rather vain: he cares for Trotsky and thinks a deal of him, so much, indeed, that at moments this foolhardy fighter becomes accessible to doubt and fear. He enjoys power and has a sense of humour, and the humour of power seems to appeal to him almost as much as its responsibility (this also fits him admirably for dealing with European Chancelleries). There is nothing of the pathos about him which attached to Kerensky, the Hamlet of the Russian Revolution. He will make himself respected, men shall reckon with him, the world must not forget Trotsky or leave him out of account. He imposes himself on it by his cleverness and energy. These qualities have served him well with crowds and with women. To vain men no one can replace success on the wider stage so well as women; they are the perfect audience for "Kings in Babylon."

Trotsky has been poor all his life. He has lived in garrets, has starved, and yet has thought of how the world should be ruled. He knows what life is to those cast into the outer darkness. Easeful pleasure is suited for men who safely possess; destruction is the instinct, the living art and the wild joy of the dispossessed—the dark, cynical, defiant face of Michael Angelo's statue of Brutus menaces the exquisite and aristocratic beauty of Leonardo da Vinci. As Trotsky has been poor all his life, the usual stories are now told of his having been bribed by the Germans. "German agent" is the most appropriate label for anyone who does not suit us. The curse of being a politician and poor is temptation, and next, that even if the man resists temptation, there is circumstantial evidence to suggest the opposite. The only temptation which approaches the rich politician and to which he duly succumbs is that of giving bribes—he "nurses" his constituency, subscribes to party funds, ends by buying hereditary legislative power in the House of Lords, and remains "respectable—damned respectable."

Trotsky achieved prominence for the first time during the revolution of 1905. Nosar ("party name": Hrustalev), an insignificant person, was chairman of the Central Soviet. Trotsky, his assistant, supplied the brains of the movement, and it was with him that the Prime Minister, Count Witte, negotiated previous to the publication of the October Manifesto. After the collapse of the revolution, Trotsky sought refuge abroad and relapsed into comparative obscurity. Unequalled as an agitator, a speaker, a man of action, Trotsky is not the leader for a persecuted creed, who could fortify them in their devout prayers in the Catacombs, or—to give the Russian-Socialist equivalent—take part with all seriousness in their sterile discussions in exile. Trotsky's Socialism is sincere, his very temperament is revolutionary Socialism, he is carried away by it. He thinks through his temperament. In the white heat of abstract passion he sees issues with a logical consistency such as cannot be attained in the everyday perception of reality, when comparatively small accidents of environment compete with the ideas which are the work of the speculative human understanding. To Trotsky Socialism and its creed have become his world, and he could hardly live or act outside their sphere. But the theoretical differences between the various Socialist groups were unessential to him at a time when as yet none of their doctrines could give rise to action. His restless ambition, his excitable temper, his desire for action, made him shift from one Socialist group to another, while blind zeal and lack of humour made other men persevere and attain leadership. Trotsky finished by being called "the morass" by those strong in faith—the uncertain, dangerous ground between the immovable mountains.

August 1914 found him in Paris. His first move was an attack on the German Socialists for having voted war-credits. During the next two years he edited a Russian Socialist paper. Towards the end of 1916 the French Government, to disembarrass itself of Trotsky, decided to put him across the Swiss frontier; it seemed that there he would remain high and dry till the end of the war. He succeeded, however, in getting himself sent to Spain instead, and thence embarked for America. To one born in bondage, chained in his youth, exiled in his manhood, the Revolution of 1917 was the sign that the days of sterile misery had come to an end. Not yet! By order of the British authorities Trotsky was forcibly taken off a homeward-bound Norwegian steamer and interned at Halifax. Those few weeks of detention in Nova Scotia did not kill him; but, as Machiavelli puts it—*si vendicano gli uomini delle leggiere offese; delle gravi non possono.*[9] The remembrance of wrong done to his own person rendered more pointed Trotsky's action for the release of Chicherin. Yet the first document compromising to the German Government which he selected for publication was a letter from the Kaiser to the Tsar, complaining of the asylum accorded to revolutionaries in Great Britain, and proposing joint representations on that subject. Trotsky thus reminded his comrades of the time when Prussia had offered itself as an assistant to their hangmen, and Prince Bülow sneered at "Silberfarb" and "Mandelstamm"! Not even our most God-forsaken official underlings with a flair for the psychological moment when petty chicanery creates the maximum of irritation can altogether wipe out the memory of those other days.

The pre-revolutionary opposition in the Duma was political; the

[9] Men are punished for slight offenses, but little is done to them who commit grave ones.

revolution which broke out in the streets, social. The Cadets aimed at constitutional reform and at a more efficient prosecution of the war. They could not give the sign for active revolt, lest it should interfere with the conduct of the war. The revolution was made by men to whom the war was not the first concern. The Cadets joined it after the day was won. The peasantry and army cried out for land and peace. The Cadets desired to go on with the war till victory was won, and to check social revolution. These were two irreconcilable programmes. Kerensky tried to reconcile them. He wanted all classes to unite, to offer sacrifices and to have confidence in each other. The masses were to submit to the leadership and discipline of the educated bourgeoisie, suffer yet further in a war of which they hardly understood the meaning, and trust to the upper classes not to use in future their regained power for preventing the social revolution. The upper classes were to work cheerfully, viewing with equanimity the certain doom in store for them on the conclusion of peace. Kerensky's endeavours were met with opposition, nay, with direct sabotage, from the Right and the Left, and with scant understanding among the Western Allies. His attempt broke down.

Then came Trotsky's day and burden. With him and the Bolsheviks the strangest factor has entered the war—a belligerent power to whom war on national lines has neither sense nor meaning. The only war which they understand is between classes, and that war knows no frontiers. It is not peace which they carry to the world, but strife; they are militants, but in a different dimension. Could Trotsky raise, arm and officer a sufficiently big army he would menace, not the Central Powers alone, but all the bourgeois Governments of the world; though he would probably try to avoid fighting their armies in battles which indiscriminately sacrifice bourgeois and proletarians. He naturally demands complete self-determination for all nationalities throughout the world—which implies, among other things, the end of German imperialism, the complete disruption of the Habsburg Monarchy and of the Turkish Empire (one has to come to England to find Socialists or "democrats" who, from sheer controversial perversity, become champions of such dynastic creations!). But to Trotsky self-determination is merely one aspect of a much wider problem. "Why should people object so strongly to the dominion of one nation over another," the Bolshevik would say, "and yet within the same nation admit that one man should be born in economic subjection to another man? Why talk about 'submerged nationalities' and be silent about submerged classes?" To the Bolsheviks the different ideas of possession and dominion are but parts of one organic whole of which the vital nerve may be destroyed by a violent blow, but which it is almost impossible to transform by degrees. Evolution comes after revolution to eliminate the moribund forms by a gradual process. That is why systems survive revolutions, and yet cannot be killed apart from revolution. As Hartmann put it in 1848, referring to the constitutional problem raised by the French Revolution—

> Das ist der Zeiten bittere Not,
> Der Widerspruch der schwer zu heben,
> Dass die Monarchie wohl tot,
> Aber die Monarchen leben.[10]

Most of Trotsky's ideas are incomprehensible to the illiterate masses in the armies and peasantry of Russia which have raised him to power. They want peace because they are tired of fighting, not because they hold any particular views on international relations. They desire to expropriate the rich without any clear idea of the condition which is to supplant the order they destroy. The immense, almost inconceivable, suffering inflicted on the Russian peasant-soldier during the first three years of the war by the criminal callousness and corruption of the *ancien régime* has resulted in a psychological catastrophe—a disappearance of military and social discipline unequalled in history, and a collapse of routine and tradition, the framework of everyday life. The intellectual revolutionaries sail in the storm, and their sails rise over the waves, in appearance a triumphant sign of the storm itself. Yet they have no real control over the blind elemental forces which cannot be disciplined, least of all by the revolutionaries themselves. For if Trotsky tried to coerce them and succeeded in that attempt—which in reality is impossible—he would break the very spirit and force of the revolution. He is not the man for such work.

Without an army at his command, with a country plunged in anarchy and demanding peace, with masses only very dimly comprehending the meaning of the events which now unfold, Trotsky has to face the Teutonic Powers (January 1918). It would seem that he is at their mercy. And yet a dark fear haunts his opponents.

[10] This is the time's bitter need,/ The contrast which is difficult to do away with,/ That monarchy is dead,/ But the monarchs still live.

There is the suffering and despair of their own peoples, their crav-
ing for peace, their rage, which, hitherto silent, may any moment
burst out in a desperate cry. They, too, have heard the watchword
about "the rule of the downtrodden" and "the turn of the wheel."
It is to them that Trotsky speaks over the heads of their rulers.
What do the starving German masses care for dominion over other
races? Has not enough blood been shed? Are the maimed and
crippled too few in number? Trotsky speaks sincerely about peace.
Russia sets all her nations free. She threatens nobody. If peace
negotiations break down, will anyone believe that it was through
Russia's fault? German and Austrian statesmen wriggle, they ma-
noeuvre for positions; they make the most amazing professions of
principle and contradict them in the same breath, they try to set
themselves right in the eyes of their peoples. Trotsky unmasks their
game and analyses aloud each move they make. The scene is almost grotesque. As Dr. Harold Williams put it in one of his Petrograd despatches, the Germans "are in the position of the mediaeval
knight, playing a weird game of chess with supernatural powers."

If the war continues, what can the German Government do? Can
it risk ordering its armies across the undefended Russian front? Will
they obey? Will they attack the country which was the first to offer
peace? Perhaps. But if the Germans get to Russia—again, what
can they do? They cannot coerce Russia. Revolutionary Russia is
already a nightmare to them, and even from their own country
Germany's rulers cannot eliminate any more the forces and ideas
which the war has set in motion.

10
Trotsky in the Struggle for Power

    Friction between Trotsky and several of the "old Bolsheviks" can be traced back to a series of disagreements which emerged during the Civil War. Then, these disagreements appeared as the inevitable squabbles arising from the heat of battle; in no way did they seem to foretell the fierce encounter which was to follow. It was Lenin's illness and death in 1924 which signaled the commencement of the struggle for power between Trotsky and Stalin. Since the nature of the rivalry between the two leaders of the Revolution remains, to this day, a highly controversial question, the following extracts are not intended as an explanation of what the controversy was about (that question is treated in the concluding Part of this book). Rather, they enable us to gauge Trotsky's popularity in the mid-twenties, to observe his behavior in the struggle, and to examine the nature of Stalinist arguments employed against him.

    William Reswick (1890–1954) was born in the Ukraine and then emigrated to the United States. He graduated from the New York University Law School in 1919, and then achieved considerable success as a journalist, serving as Chief of the Moscow Bureau for Associated Press. There he met many prominent Bolsheviks, and was in a position to chronicle the vicissitudes of their political careers. The excerpt from Reswick's book I Dreamt Revolution *shows how effectively Stalin controlled the party, and Trotsky's disadvantage on entering the fray. Reswick also describes how Trotsky was associated, in the minds of many, with the idea of "world revolution," and, more ominously, with Bonapartism—military dictatorship. His concluding passage underlines Trotsky's continuing popularity with the masses after Lenin's death.*

    Max Eastman, a prominent American socialist in his earlier years, had helped to establish and edit The Masses *(1911) and then* The Liberator *(1919). During the twenties he spent considerable time in the Soviet Union and came to know Trotsky well. He was one of the first foreigners in Russia to learn of Lenin's will and its stern condemnation of Stalin. His book, Since Lenin Died, was a courageous attempt to explain the baffling nature of the struggle for power which was being waged in Soviet Russia. It provides important insight into Trotsky's personality, insight which is certainly contrary to the estimates of other writers.*

The remaining selections are by Zinoviev, Stalin, and the official pronouncements of the History of the Communist Party of the Soviet Union (B). *The Zinoviev and Stalin selections should be compared with the earlier evaluations of Radek and Lunacharsky. Beginning in the winter of 1923, every effort was made to minimize Trotsky's historic role, to vilify his character, and to convince both Russian masses and foreign communists that Trotsky's dedicated purpose was and had been to destroy the Bolshevik Party and to sabotage the construction of socialism in the Soviet Union.*

FOREIGN OBSERVERS

William Reswick[1]

During those hopeful winter months very little was heard either of Stalin or of Trotsky. But shortly after Easter (1924) a series of alarming rumors shook the capital. The most persistent was to the effect that Lenin's testament had demanded the removal of Stalin as Secretary of the Communist Party. That testament, people averred, was sacred. To ignore it seemed convincing proof that Stalin, despite his yielding to the Moderates, was all-powerful in the inner councils of the party.

In support of this argument some competent observers stressed the appointment of Frunze, a known Stalinist, as Vice-Commissar of War. Of far greater significance was a decision by the Politburo to check every order of War Commissar Trotsky, no matter how routine. Obviously, the intriguing trio—Stalin, Zinoviev, Kamenev —were still active behind the scenes. But to what extent? That question remained unanswered for some time.

By chance I got a behind-the-scene glimpse of the real political setup. I was just about to set out for a visit to my family in France when Bradford Merrill cabled me instructions to interview Trotsky.

[1] From William Reswick, *I Dreamt Revolution* (Chicago: Henry Regnery Company, 1952), pp. 77–80, 120, 150–52. Reprinted by permission of the publisher.

Rothstein, head of the Soviet Press Department, dismissed the request abruptly. Such an interview, he warned, might imperil my chances of obtaining a return visa to Russia.

Ignoring the warning, I asked Sasha to make the appointment. He did it on one condition. I was to refrain from any questions concerning the Apparat. Anything connected with Stalin's secretariat must be avoided because the relations between the War Commissar and the Secretary of the party were growing worse daily.

At the War Office on Znamyenka I found Trotsky cheerful and seemingly in good health. Much to my surprise he ignored Sasha's condition to steer clear of party issues. In answer to my first question, what he thought of the prospects of NEP, Trotsky attacked the triumvirate, charging them with numerous attempts to liquidate Lenin's New Economic Policy. At the same time he praised Rykov for his devotion to Leninism in economic matters. He stressed the word "economic," adding, off the record, that he and the Premier did not see eye to eye on foreign policy. Reverting to NEP, Trotsky said: "The New Economic Policy may have saved the Revolution. It surely prevented a second, perhaps a fatal, famine." Trotsky then switched from NEP to the question of granting foreign concessions, stressing its importance to Russia's industry. He compared the Soviet industrial task with that of the United States during the World War, saying: "What we need here is an organizer like Bernard M. Baruch."

Trotsky's keen interest in this topic seemed to me, at the moment, a convenient way of evading further talk about the troika. I learned later that at the time of our talk the War Commissar already knew of his eventual demotion and appointment to the humble office of chairman of the Commission on Foreign Concessions.

My interview with Trotsky took place in the early evening, and it was only in parting that he informed me he would have to read my copy before I could send it to New York. He rang for his secretary, who offered to call for the copy at the Hotel Savoy, where I was stopping, and return it later in the evening. We arranged that everything, including the censor's OK, should be ready by midnight, Moscow time.

Trotsky's secretary called for my copy at nine o'clock but failed to return an hour later as agreed. I waited for him until midnight, when New York came through with an urgent query. For two hours I tried vainly to contact Trotsky. There was no way of reaching him. Sasha, too, had vanished. Finally I called at the War Office.

After many excuses Trotsky's secretary told me the interview was being held up by the party censor. It was the first time I ever heard of a censor outside and above the one at the Foreign Office. Seeming eager to help me, the secretary promised to bring the copy shortly. Then he, too, vanished, and I was left hanging in the air between the mysterious censor at the Kremlin and my anxious editors.

A stranger telephoned at four in the morning. He demanded to know whether I was Grazhdanin (Citizen) Reswick.

"Your interview with Comrade Trotsky," said the voice, "had to be translated into Russian. You will find it at Chicherin's secretariat."

At the Foreign Office, Chicherin's chief assistant handed me two pages typed in Russian. They were the mangled remains of my story, a mere ghost of the original.

Chicherin, the kindhearted Foreign Commissar, was still at his desk. I showed him the copy. Dead tired after a night's toil, he glanced at the poorly typed pages and mumbled: "You ought to be glad they left you anything at all to cable. It could have been worse."

Out in the typist's room, while translating the Russian back into English, Chicherin's secretary informed me that the party censor had telephoned to the Foreign Commissar earlier.

"Comrade Chicherin," he said, "barely managed to save you these two pages."

This experience at the War Office was my first evidence that the Stalin-Trotsky fight was on again.

The interview filed, I was free to take my leave, and after a few hours sleep I got busy packing. Sasha showed up at the station, where he informed me that Trotsky was distressed over the incident. As the train moved away, I saw tears in my friend's eyes.

"Good-by, Volodya," he called after me. "God knows whether we shall ever meet again." . . .

The Kremlin chimes rang out midnight. About to leave, I asked the Premier whether the prospects of a truly democratic Soviet Union were as bright now as they had seemed to him on the day when he took office. Rykov's reply remains in memory, a poignant reminder of Stalin's rare talent for confusing and disarming his adversaries.

"We must choose," Rykov said, "between a probability and a dead certainty. Stalin may or may not be aiming for dictatorship, but it is certain that Trotsky's determination to make Russia a center of world revolution will in the long run bring us to war and destruction. And there is the additional likelihood of one of Trotsky's military geniuses like Tukhachevsky becoming a Russian Napoleon."

Thus, despite their knowledge that Stalin was a growing menace, Rykov and his friends refused to join hands with Trotsky—a step which at that time would have resulted in Stalin's quick and painless removal. Like the leaders of the world's great democracies during World War II, the Moderates in the Kremlin were beguiled by Stalin's maneuvers, his consummate acting, his genius for deceit, his promises which he would keep scrupulously so long as a show of good faith helped to further his hidden designs. Although they knew all about his underhand activities in the secretariat, the Rights, and even some of the leading Trotskyists, were taken in by Stalin's adroitness in exploiting the menace of counterrevolution. His ultimate weapon in every crisis was a timely reminder that the alternative to a dictated unity was to hang separately on Tsarist gallows.

That night, despite Rykov's abiding optimism, I had a premonition of impending tragedy. For the moment I could not help blaming both the Rights and the Trotskyists for their failure to act while there was still time. It took Yalta and Potsdam to give me an adequate perception of the astute politician those idealists were up against. . . .

In pursuing this policy Rykov's group compromised much of their original program. After three years in power they were still unable to agree as to the lesser of the two evils confronting Russia: a dictatorship by Trotsky, or one by Stalin. To many Moderates in the party Trotsky seemed the greater menace, if only because of his overwhelming appeal to the masses.

The more I observed the scene, the firmer grew my belief that downright jealousy of Trotsky's rare talents was of tremendous help to the cold, calculating Stalin as he proceeded to weave his far-reaching web of intrigue. On the platform and in the press, opposition to Trotsky remained on a high level of theoretic debate, but in private talk nearly every leader betrayed a deep-rooted envy that befogged his vision. Men who had spent the greater part of their lives in prison or exile, idealists who had given their all in a great cause, the bolshevik leaders with but few exceptions seemed invulnerable to human temptations—save applause and acclaim, which they loved above all else in life.

One day in the autumn of 1926 the Moscow soviet staged a

demonstration against the threat of the British Merchant Marine to boycott Soviet ports. That would have meant a renewal of Russia's economic isolation, a menace so grave as to call for an immediate and striking show of Soviet unity in the face of peril.

On my way to the rally I was struck by the sight of streets crowded with men, women, and children instead of the usual columns marching under orders. The big hall was packed with civilians, Red Army men, and sailors. The foremost leaders of the party and government were on the platform—all except Trotsky. Yet the man's name was on everybody's lips. I heard it in the streets, on the square fronting the Moscow soviet, and inside the hall. The immense crowd, it was quite obvious, had come there to greet the former Commissar of War, who had not appeared in public since his demotion to Commissar of Foreign Concessions. For the first time Moscow had an opportunity to show its resentment against Stalin's machinations, and the people turned out en masse, eager to demonstrate.

It was five in the afternoon on a bright, clear day when the meeting was opened in Trotsky's absence. After some brief remarks the chairman began to introduce the speakers. One by one they came to the stand, spoke their lines, and were mildly applauded. Among the notables on the platform were Rykov, Stalin, Yenukidze, Kamenev, Zinoviev, Lunacharsky, and Bukharin. They all, except Stalin and Zinoviev, took their turn in telling the audience what they thought of England's action and its dire meaning. Each speaker tried hard to whip up enthusiasm for the benefit of the foreign press. But the audience remained strangely passive. Most people in the hall were waiting for Trotsky and were in no mood to listen to anyone else.

Then, in the midst of Kamenev's speech, a distant roar came through the open windows. It rose steadily in volume and vehemence and rolled like the thunder of an approaching storm. Presently it drowned out Kamenev's voice and, as he stood there vainly gesticulating, Trotsky appeared on the platform. Instantly the audience turned into a howling, swaying, screaming mass. Men jumped on chairs. Soldiers and sailors hurled their caps to the vaulted ceiling. For over fifteen minutes they cried, laughed, yelled, and blew kisses at their idol. For a time it seemed as if nothing could stop the uproar.

Trotsky tried hard to calm the crowd. But the more he tried, the greater seemed their determination to go on cheering. As at the Grand Theater after the announcement of Lenin's death, I watched

the men on the platform, eager to get their reaction to this out-
burst of emotion. With but few exceptions, every face on the platform betrayed resentment, anger, and consuming envy. Rykov and
Yenukidze were the only ones who took the demonstration with
genial good grace. They waved to the wildly cheering soldiers and
joined in the applause for their wartime leader. Stalin was expres-
sionless. At rare intervals he would exchange glances with Yenukidze
sitting next to him.

After the cheers finally died down Trotsky began his speech.
He started without being presented by the chairman. To introduce
him seemed as superfluous as to introduce a tornado. As I listened to
Trotsky it occurred to me that for the first time in all those years I
could sense the glory and pathos of the Revolution. It was my first
opportunity to hear the great tribune, whose flaming word had sent
defeated regiments back to battle and victory.

Years before, in New York, I had heard orators like William
Jennings Bryan, Woodrow Wilson, and others. But Trotsky was
without a peer. He was a virtuoso of speech, a master of oratory
who could play on the heartstrings of men with the ease and grace
of a great violinist. In a few minutes he had the crowd hypnotized.
They cheered, laughed, cried, responding to the speaker's every mood
and gesture. As Trotsky, heartened by the tremendous response, rose
to ever greater heights of appeal, his colleagues on the platform
seemed to shrivel and fade in the shadows of the poorly lighted
stage. Seeing this dwarfed Politburo, I could well understand the
oft-repeated assertion that Trotsky, even more than Lenin, had
engineered the Revolution, snatched it from mortal peril on the
fields of battle, and saved the bolshevik leaders from the gallows.
Yet there remained little gratitude among them for their savior,
and much hatred and envy. To the people, roaring inside and outside the hall, Trotsky was still the hero of October. That very fact,
however, made him a menace to his less popular comrades.

Max Eastman[2]

A legend has been created and carefully nourished by those now
in power in Russia that Trotsky attempted to use his popularity,
after Lenin's death, in order to maneuvre himself into a position
of leadership that Lenin did not want him to have. The fact that

[2] From Max Eastman, *Since Lenin Died* (New York: Boni & Liveright, 1925),
pp. 17–19, 93–96. Copyright © 1925 by Boni & Liveright, Inc. Reprinted by permission of the publisher.

Lenin urged upon Trotsky his place at the head of the Government, and that Trotsky declined it, completely discredits this legend. But it leaves a perplexing question in its place. Why did Trotsky decline the elevated position which Lenin offered him? The correct answer to that question will give you the key to everything that follows. He declined it because he has no idea whatever of personal political maneuvring. He has nothing but a complete incapacity for it. He is not only unable to play this game for personal motives, but he is unable to play it when his most impersonal ideals demand that he should. He knows how to fight his enemies, but he does not know how to manage his friends. He does not know how to manipulate men. He has no impulse to do it. He never thinks of it. That is his great weakness.

If Trotsky had appeared at the first break as Lenin's substitute, the whole party and the whole world would have been set right about their relations, and more than half of what has happened would have been impossible; and certainly any man consciously entering a struggle for power would have grabbed this first and obviously essential strategic moment. Trotsky was incapable of seeing his duty as a struggle for personal power within the party. He was incapable of living the life of the party in those terms. "An intellectual struggle within the party," he said once, "does not mean mutual rejection, but mutual influence." And he continued to act upon this maxim after Lenin withdrew, although it then quite obviously ceased to be true. Stalin and Zinoviev and Kamenev had already, at the very beginning of Lenin's decline, formed a block against Trotsky in the Politburo, the ruling committee of the party. Trotsky was in a continual minority there at the source of power. He knew that he would be baulked at every point as the head of the Government. He knew, I suppose, his own inability to wheedle and coax. He is a natural commander. The situation was complicated, moreover, by his disagreement with Lenin upon that fundamental question of "Government planning," upon which Lenin subsequently yielded to him. All this would have made no difference if he had seen the situation as the "triumvirate" saw it—as a struggle for power in the future. He saw it as an impossible situation in the present. And with a quixotic objectiveness which is far harder to understand than calculating ambition, he declined Lenin's proposal that he should become the head of the Soviet Government, and thus of the revolutionary movement of the world. That peculiar reaction—an over-correction, perhaps, of the personal egotism which would dominate a simpler man in such a situation—does not command my admiration. I think it is a misfortune, but it is the fact about Trotsky's action at this time, and about his character in general. And without understanding this fact and this character you will not understand the events that followed.

This act of Trotsky's was simply an invitation to his enemies to perfect and solidify the block which they had already formed against him among the leaders of the party. With Stalin—who possesses all the craftiness that Trotsky lacks—in the key position as secretary of the party, and with Zinoviev enthusiastically cooperating, Kamenev not unwilling, and Bucharin easy to influence, they proceeded, by all those subtle means which the reader understands, to build up an efficient political machine for grabbing and holding the power within the party. The ideology which served them in building up this fractional machine in a party in which fractions are forbidden, was that Trotsky is a potential Bonaparte—or a potential Danton, there was some disagreement about this at the beginning!—and that the revolution must be saved from the danger involved in his popularity.

There are two mistakes which you can make here. One is to imagine that this fractional machine was not deliberately built up, and built up for this specific purpose. The other is to imagine that mere personal ambition was the motive to it. These men were undoubtedly aided by their own thirst of power in arriving at the conviction that they were the true Bolsheviks, and that there was something fundamentally wrong with Trotsky. But the conviction was nevertheless sincere and profound. It is largely explained by the fact that Trotsky stands so high above all the others, both in intellect and self-dependent force, that if he gained an ascendant influence, he would inevitably occupy a position similar to that of Lenin. . . .

You will wonder how it could have been possible, by such obvious tricks, to beat Trotsky down from his great height, and grab the whole power out of his hands. One thing that goes a little way toward explaining it is the peculiar reaction of Trotsky himself. Since the stampede was produced by a campaign of subtle and plausible misrepresentation on the part of men whom the party had learned to trust, the only thing which could have checked it, would have been an act of transcendant candour on Trotsky's part. He would have had to find a way to put forth his whole real warm and convincing personality in a deliberate response to a deliberate personal attack. He would have had to make the entire party feel that they knew him personally, and could, therefore, personally deny what they were being told. But his pride led him in the opposite direction. So far as the articles in Pravda were not replies to his words, but a deliberate falsification of them, he made no answer whatever. He not only made no answer to this enormous polemical and calumnious outpouring, which filled all Russia for half the winter, but he never read any of it. I asked him once why he did not take all these issues of Pravda, and retire for a week, and analyse them and write a complete factual explanation of the whole thing.

"Why, this is not an argument, it is a personal attack," he said, "I can't reply to a thing like that." And he spread out his hands as though this proposition were perfectly obvious.

To me it did not seem obvious, and I continued:

"Now, you could take that speech of Stalin's about 'The Six Mistakes of Comrade Trotsky,' for instance. . . ."

"What is that?" he asked, and he smiled at my expression. "I haven't read any of those things," he explained.

I murmured my amazement, and he spread his hands again in that gesture which indicates that something is quite obvious.

"Why should I read what they write?" he said. "They aren't discussing anything that I said. There is no misunderstanding."

That is the way Trotsky talked to his friends. But throughout the height of this panic he was ill in the Caucasus, and even those few conversations for which he finds time in the pressure of his work were impossible. And in his published writings he maintained an impersonal dignity and objectivity that might in ordinary times be admirable. The self-command and perfect equilibrium revealed by it were admirable. But as a reaction to an attack, it was not intelligible to simple people. It played directly into the hands of those who were propagating calumnious legends about him. It made him seem remote, and a little mysterious, and very sharply different from Lenin, who so often cleared the air by the simple device of saying all that he thought.

I talked once about Trotsky with the man into whose family he moved at the age of nine, when he left home to go to school in Odessa. And the first thing that man said in answer to my questioning, was: "We did not really know what Leon Davidovitch was thinking about—even at that age he was so perfectly self-contained."

In my own acquaintance with Trotsky I have observed this same quality, and found it irritating. He has that part of a social nature which consists of listening with sympathetic attention while you explain yourself, but he has not that part which consists of instinctively explaining himself. He is extremely frank—quite startling in that respect—but you have to ask him questions. As I have said, the most significant part of his speech before the party Congress was his offer to answer "any questions whatever" that the delegates might ask him. And I notice that in his letter resigning his post in the Red Army he repeated this proposal. He had remained in Moscow, although ordered south by his physicians, in order to be able to "answer this or that question or make any necessary explanations." Again, of course, no explanations were asked for. Nothing has been more precious to his enemies, and more essential to their success, than this poised reticence of Trotsky's, his lack of that irresistible impulse which most of us have to explain ourselves.

Trotsky said, in the note inserted in Pravda which I have already quoted, that he refrained from answering these personal attacks because he believed it was to the best interests of the party. And in his letter of resignation he asserted that he still believed "his silence had been right from the standpoint of the general interests of the party." In attributing his absolute silence to his temperament, I do not mean to deny that he exercised this judgment and acted upon it. Moreover, in so far as the true answer to the attack upon him consisted of laying bare the facts that I have stated here, it would be bold under the existing circumstances to question his judgment. The thing which I attribute to his temperament is the absoluteness of his silence. A man who was not proud and had a strong impulse toward social self-expression, would not have acted upon a rigid principle here. He would have found a way to make the party feel the response of his personality without violating its discipline or breaking its solidarity before the world. At least, that is my opinion. And I believe that Trotsky himself might have found this more practical course if he had been able to appear in public at the beginning of the stampede. Nobody can tell how much his sickness played into the hands of his enemies. It is certain that they consciously reckoned upon it in starting this unscrupulous campaign.

THE ANTI-TROTSKY CAMPAIGN

Zinoviev[3]

The last attack of Comrade Trotsky (the "Lessons of October")
is nothing else than a fairly open attempt to revise—or even directly to liquidate—the foundation of Leninism. It will only require a short time and this will be plain to the whole of our Party
and to the whole International. The "novelty" in this attempt consists in the fact that, out of "strategical" considerations, it is attempted to carry out this revision in the name of Lenin.

We experienced something similar at the beginning of the campaign of Bernstein and his followers, when they began the "revision" of the foundation of Marxism. The ideas of Marx were already so generally recognised in the international labour movement,
that even their revision, at least at the beginning, had to be undertaken in the name of Marx. A quarter of a century was necessary
before the revisionists could finally throw aside their mask and
openly pronounce that, in the field of theory, they had entirely
broken away from Marx. This took place in a most open manner, in
literature, only in the year 1924 in the recently published collection
of articles devoted to the 70th birthday of Kautsky.

The ideas of Leninism at present predominate to such an extent
in the international revolutionary movement—and particularly in
our country—that the "critics" of Leninism consider it necessary to
have recourse to similar methods. They undertake the revision of
Leninism "in the name of Lenin," citing Lenin, emphasising their
fidelity to the principles of Leninism. This "strategy" however does
not help. It is already seen through by the Leninist Party. It only
needs a few weeks, and all the sparrows on the house-tops will be
twittering over the collapse of this remarkable strategy. Comrade
Trotsky has overlooked one trifle: that our Party is so Leninist and
so mature that it is capable of distinguishing Leninism from Trotskyism.

The attack of Comrade Trotsky is an attack with inadequate
means. Nobody will succeed in liquidating the foundations of Leninism, or carrying out even a partial revision of the principles of
Leninism, or even succeed in getting Trotskyism recognised as a
"justifiable tendency" within Leninism. Nobody will succeed in

[3] From *The Errors of Trotskyism* (London: Communist Party of Great Britain,
1925), pp. 166–68; 171–72. Reprinted by permission of the publisher.

convincing the Party that we now need some sort of synthesis of Leninism and Trotskyism. Trotskyism is as fit to be a constituent part of Leninism as a spoonful of tar can be a constituent part of a vat of honey. . . .

If Lenin is the classical type of the proletarian revolutionary, Trotsky is the "classical" type of the intellectual revolutionary. The latter has, of course, certain strong features he succeeds sometimes in combining with the proletariat mass, but that which forms the nature of his political activity is the intellectual revolutionarism.

We give below a compressed political description of the life of Trotskyism which possesses the authority of coming from the pen of Lenin:

"He, Trotsky, was in the year 1903 a Menshevik, left this Party in 1904, returned to the Mensheviki in 1905 and paraded round with ultra-revolutionary phrases. In 1906 he again abandoned this Party; at the end of 1906 he again defended the election alliance with the cadets and in the spring of 1907 he stated at the London Conference that the difference between him and Rosa Luxemburg rather constituted a difference of individual shades of opinion than a difference of political tendency. To-day Trotsky borrows some ideas from the one fraction and to-morrow from the other, and, therefore, considers himself as a man standing above both fractions." (Lenin's Collected Works, vol. xi, part 2, pp. 308–309.)

"Never in a single serious question of Marxism has Trotsky had a firm opinion, he always squeezes himself in a division between this or that difference of opinion and always runs from one side to the other. At present he is in the company of the 'Bund' and of the liquidators."

Thus wrote Lenin in an article in the revue "Enlightenment," published in 1914.

"However well meant the intentions of Martov and Trotsky may be subjectively, objectively they support by their tolerance Russian imperialism."

Thus wrote Lenin in the "Socialdemokrat" No. 1, October, 1916. . . .

Stalin[4]

a) Among these legends must be included also the very widespread story that Trotsky was the "sole" or "chief organiser" of the

---

[4] From Joseph Stalin, *Works* (Moscow: Foreign Language Publishing House, 1953–55), Vol. VI, pp. 350–52.

victories on the fronts of the civil war. I must declare, comrades, in the interest of truth, that this version is quite out of accord with the facts. I am far from denying that Trotsky played an important role in the civil war. But I must emphatically declare that the high honour of being the organiser of our victories belongs not to individuals, but to the great collective body of advanced workers in our country, the Russian Communist Party. Perhaps it will not be out of place to quote a few examples. You know that Kolchak and Denikin were regarded as the principal enemies of the Soviet Republic. You know that our country breathed freely only after those enemies were defeated. Well, history shows that both these enemies, i.e., Kolchak and Denikin, were routed by our troops in spite of Trotsky's plans.

Judge for yourselves.

1) Kolchak. This is in the summer of 1919. Our troops are advancing against Kolchak and are operating near Ufa. A meeting of the Central Committee is held. Trotsky proposes that the advance be halted along the line of the River Belaya (near Ufa), leaving the Urals in the hands of Kolchak, and that part of the troops be withdrawn from the Eastern Front and transferred to the Southern Front. A heated debate takes place. The Central Committee disagrees with Trotsky, being of the opinion that the Urals, with its factories and railway network, must not be left in the hands of Kolchak, for the latter could easily recuperate there, organise a strong force and reach the Volga again; Kolchak must first be driven beyond the Ural range into the Siberian steppes, and only after that has been done should forces be transferred to the South. The Central Committee rejects Trotsky's plan. Trotsky hands in his resignation. The Central Committee refuses to accept it. Commander-in-Chief Vatsetis, who supported Trotsky's plan, resigns. His place is taken by a new Commander-in-Chief, Kamenev. From that moment Trotsky ceases to take a direct part in the affairs of the Eastern Front.

2) Denikin. This is in the autumn of 1919. The offensive against Denikin is not proceeding successfully. The "steel ring" around Mamontov (Mamontov's raid) is obviously collapsing. Denikin captures Kursk. Denikin is approaching Orel. Trotsky is summoned from the Southern Front to attend a meeting of the Central Committee. The Central Committee regards the situation as alarming and decides to send new military leaders to the Southern Front and to withdraw Trotsky. The new military leaders demand "no in-

tervention" by Trotsky in the affairs of the Southern Front. Trotsky ceases to take a direct part in the affairs of the Southern Front. Operations on the Southern Front, right up to the capture of Rostov-on-Don and Odessa by our troops, proceed without Trotsky. Let anybody try to refute these facts.

b)[5] The Party holds that our revolution is a socialist revolution, that the October Revolution is not merely a signal, an impulse, a point of departure for the socialist revolution in the West, but that at the same time it is, firstly, a base for the further development of the world revolutionary movement, and, secondly, it ushers in a period of transition from capitalism to socialism in the U.S.S.R. (dictatorship of the proletariat), during which the proletariat, if it pursues a correct policy towards the peasantry, can and will successfully build a complete socialist society, provided, of course, the power of the international revolutionary movement, on the one hand, and the power of the proletariat of the U.S.S.R., on the other, are great enough to protect the U.S.S.R. from armed imperialist intervention.

Trotskyism holds an entirely different view of the character and prospects of our revolution. In spite of the fact that in October 1917 the Trotskyists marched together with the Party, they held, and still hold, that in itself, and by its very nature, our revolution is not a socialist one; that the October Revolution is merely a signal, an impulse, a point of departure for the socialist revolution in the West; that if the world revolution is delayed and a victorious socialist revolution in the West does not come about in the very near future, proletarian power in Russia is bound to fall or to degenerate (which is one and the same thing) under the impact of inevitable clashes between the proletariat and the peasantry.

Whereas the Party, in organising the October Revolution, held that "the victory of socialism is possible first in several or even in one capitalist country taken separately," and that "the victorious proletariat of that country, having expropriated the capitalists and organised socialist production," can and should stand up "against the rest of the world, the capitalist world, attracting to its cause the oppressed classes of other countries, raising revolts in those countries against the capitalists, and in the event of necessity coming out even with armed force against the exploiting classes and their states" (Lenin, Vol. XVIII, pp. 232–33)—the Trotskyists, on the

[5] *Ibid.*, Vol. VIII, pp. 227–30.

other hand, although they cooperated with the Bolsheviks in the October period, held that "it would be hopeless to think . . . that, for example, a revolutionary Russia could hold out in the face of a conservative Europe" (Trotsky, Vol. III, Part 1, p. 90, Peace Programme, first published in August 1917).

Whereas our Party holds that the Soviet Union possesses "all that is necessary and sufficient" "for the building of a complete socialist society" (Lenin, On Co-operation), the Trotskyists, on the contrary, hold that "real progress of a socialist economy in Russia will become possible only after the victory of the proletariat in the major European countries" (Trotsky, Vol. III, Part 1, p. 93, "Postscript" to Peace Programme, written in 1922).

Whereas our Party holds that "ten or twenty years of correct relations with the peasantry, and victory on a world scale is assured" (Lenin, plan of the pamphlet The Tax in Kind), the Trotskyists, on the contrary, hold that the proletariat cannot have correct relations with the peasantry until the victory of the world revolution; that, having taken power, the proletariat "would come into hostile collision not only with all the bourgeois groupings which supported the proletariat during the first stages of its revolutionary struggle, but also with the broad masses of the peasantry with whose assistance it came into power," and that "the contradictions in the position of a workers' government in a backward country with an overwhelmingly peasant population can be solved only on an international scale, in the arena of the world proletarian revolution" (Trotsky, in the "Preface," written in 1922, to his book The Year 1905).

The conference notes that these views of Trotsky and his followers on the basic question of the character and prospects of our revolution are totally at variance with the views of our Party, with Leninism.

History of the Communist Party of the Soviet Union (B) [6]

What was now required was that everybody should join in the common effort, roll up his sleeves, and set to work with gusto. That is the way all who were loyal to the Party thought and acted. But not so the Trotskyites. They took advantage of the absence of

---

[6] From *History of the Communist Party of the Soviet Union (B)* (New York: International Publishers Co., Inc., 1952), pp. 264–67. Reprinted by permission of the publisher.

Lenin, who was incapacitated by grave illness, to launch a new attack on the Party and its leadership. They decided that this was a favourable moment to smash the Party and overthrow its leadership. They used everything they could as a weapon against the Party: the defeat of the revolution in Germany and Bulgaria in the autumn of 1923, the economic difficulties at home, and Lenin's illness. It was at this moment of difficulty for the Soviet state, when the Party's leader was stricken by sickness, that Trotsky started his attack on the Bolshevik Party. He mustered all the anti-Leninist elements in the Party and concocted an opposition platform against the Party, its leadership, and its policy. This platform was called the "Declaration of the Forty-Six Oppositionists." All the opposition groupings—the Trotskyites, Democratic-Centralists, and the remnants of the "Left Communist" and "Workers' Opposition" groups—united to fight the Leninist Party. In their declaration, they prophesied a grave economic crisis and the fall of the Soviet power, and demanded freedom of factions and groups as the only way out of the situation.

This was a fight for the restoration of factionalism which the Tenth Party Congress, on Lenin's proposal, had prohibited.

The Trotskyites did not make a single definite proposal for the improvement of agriculture or industry, for the improvement of the circulation of commodities, or for the betterment of the condition of the working people. This did not even interest them. The only thing that interested them was to take advantage of Lenin's absence in order to restore factions within the Party, to undermine its foundations and its Central Committee.

The platform of the forty-six was followed up by the publication of a letter by Trotsky in which he vilified the Party cadres and levelled new slanderous accusations against the Party. In this letter Trotsky harped on the old Menshevik themes which the Party had heard from him many times before.

First of all the Trotskyites attacked the Party apparatus. They knew that without a strong apparatus the Party could not live and function. The opposition tried to undermine and destroy the Party apparatus, to set the Party members against it, and the young members against the old stalwarts of the Party. In this letter Trotsky played up to the students, the young Party members who were not acquainted with the history of the Party's fight against Trotskyism. To win the support of the students, Trotsky flatteringly referred to them as the "Party's surest barometer," at the same time declaring that the Leninist old guard had degenerated. Alluding to the degeneration of the leaders of the Second International, he made the foul insinuation that the old Bolshevik guard was going the same way. By this outcry about the degeneration of the Party, Trotsky tried to hide his own degeneration and his anti-Party scheming.

The Trotskyites circulated both oppositionist documents, viz., the platform of the forty-six and Trotsky's letter, in the districts and among the Party nuclei and put them up for discussion by the Party membership.

They challenged the Party to a discussion.

Thus the Trotskyites forced a general discussion on the Party, just as they did at the time of the controversy over the trade union question before the Tenth Party Congress.

Although the Party was occupied with the far more important problems of the country's economic life, it accepted the challenge and opened the discussion.

The whole Party was involved in the discussion. The fight took a most bitter form. It was fiercest of all in Moscow, for the Trotsky-ites endeavoured above all to capture the Party organization in the capital. But the discussion was of no help to the Trotskyites. It only disgraced them. They were completely routed both in Moscow and all other parts of the Soviet Union. Only a small number of nuclei in universities and offices voted for the Trotskyites.

In January 1924 the Party held its Thirteenth Conference. The conference heard a report by Comrade Stalin, summing up the re-sults of the discussion. The conference condemned the Trotskyite opposition, declaring that it was a petty-bourgeois deviation from Marxism. The decisions of the conference were subsequently en-dorsed by the Thirteenth Party Congress and the Fifth Congress of the Communist International. The international Communist prole-tariat supported the Bolshevik Party in its fight against Trotskyism.

But the Trotskyites did not cease their subversive work. In the autumn of 1924, Trotsky published an article entitled, "The Lessons of October" in which he attempted to substitute Trotskyism for Leninism. It was a sheer slander on our Party and its leader, Lenin. This defamatory broadsheet was seized upon by all enemies of Communism and of the Soviet Government. The Party was out-raged by this unscrupulous distortion of the heroic history of Bol-shevism. Comrade Stalin denounced Trotsky's attempt to sub-stitute Trotskyism for Leninism. He declared that "it is the duty of the Party to bury Trotskyism as an ideological trend."

An effective contribution to the ideological defeat of Trotskyism and to the defense of Leninism was Comrade Stalin's theoretical work, Foundations of Leninism, published in 1924. This book is a masterly exposition and a weighty theoretical substantiation of Leninism. It was, and is today, a trenchant weapon of Marxist-Leninist theory in the hands of Bolsheviks all over the world.

In the battles against Trotskyism, Comrade Stalin rallied the Party around its Central Committee and mobilized it to carry on the fight for the victory of Socialism in our country. Comrade Stalin proved that Trotskyism had to be ideologically demolished if the further victorious advance to Socialism was to be ensured.

Reviewing this period of the fight against Trotskyism, Comrade Stalin said:

"Unless Trotskyism is defeated, it will be impossible to achieve victory under the conditions of NEP, it will be impossible to convert present-day Russia into a Socialist Russia."

11
Trotsky in Exile

The decisions reached at the XV Party Congress in December, 1927 finally led to Trotsky's exile to Alma-Ata in Soviet Central Asia. Within a short period, Stalin was able to further strengthen his position within the Party and win Politburo approval for Trotsky's expulsion from the Soviet Union. In 1929 the life of political exile began for Trotsky. He first went to Prinkipo Island, very near to Constantinople, then to Norway, and finally to Mexico.

Max Eastman's attempt to explain the nature of the power struggle between Trotsky and the Stalinists was referred to in the last chapter. This second excerpt from Eastman's work is based on his visit with Trotsky on Prinkipo Island, and is a valuable description of Trotsky at the beginning of his political wanderings.

Finally settling in Mexico, Trotsky and his followers lived under constant fear of physical attack. The household which they organized at Coyoacan, a suburb outside of Mexico City, resembled a fort under siege. Charles Cornell, who served as a bodyguard in the household, provides us with a more personal description of Trotsky's work-a-day habits.

MAX EASTMAN WITH TROTSKY ON PRINKIPO ISLAND [1]

Trotsky seems the most modest and self-forgetful of all the famous men I have known. He never boasts; he never speaks of himself or his achievements; he never monopolizes the conversation. He gives his attention freely and wholly to anything that happens or comes up. With all the weight of worldwide slander and misrepresentation he struggles under today, the peculiar position he occupies, he has not so far breathed a syllable suggestive of preoccupation with himself or even the ordinary, quite human touchiness that one might expect. As we work on his book, if I pay him a

[1] From Max Eastman, *Great Companions* (New York: Farrar, Straus & Giroux, Inc., 1959), pp. 153–69. Copyright © 1942, 1959 by Max Eastman. Reprinted by permission of the publisher.

compliment, he says some little thing, "I am glad," and then passes hastily to another subject. After all, I agree with his colleague, Lunacharsky, although I did not when I came here, that there is "not a drop of vanity in him."

Like many great men I have met he does not seem altogether robust. There is apt to be a frailty associated with great intellect. At any rate, Trotsky, especially in our heated arguments concerning the "dialectic," in which he becomes excited and wrathful to the point of losing his breath, seems to me at times almost weak. He seems too small for the struggle. He cannot laugh at my attacks on his philosophy, or be curious about them—as I imagine Lenin would —because in that field he is not secure. He is not strongly based. I get the impression of a man in unstable equilibrium because of the mountain of ability and understanding that he has to carry. In what is he unequal to the load? In self-confidence? Is it the Jew's inferiority complex after all? Is it that he has never played, never loafed and invited his soul, or observed that the sunshine is good whatever happens? When I remarked that fishing with a dragnet is interesting work, but not sport, he said:

"Two plusses—it is interesting and it is work! What more can you ask?"

I wonder if that is the mood in which he will go fishing—intense, speedy, systematic, organized for success, much as he went to Kazan to defeat the White Armies.

He seems to me over-sure of everything he believes. I suppose that is what Lenin meant in his testament when he warned the party against Trotsky's "excessive self-confidence." But I suspect that his weaker point as a political leader would be that when that cocksureness breaks down, he is non-plussed. He does not know how to cherish a doubt, how to speculate. Between us, at least, to confer is out of the question.

His magnanimity, his freedom from anything like rancour, is amazing. I see it in his portrayal of his enemies, but also in smaller things. Yesterday we reached a point of tension in our argument about dialectic that was extreme. Trotsky's throat was throbbing and his face was red; he was in a rage. His wife was worried, evidently, and when we left the tea table and went into his study still fighting, she came in after us and stood there above and beside me like a statue, silent and austere. I understood what she meant and said, after a long, hot speech from him:

"Well, let's lay aside this subject and go to work on the book."

"As much as you like!" he jerked out, and snapped up the manuscript.

I began reading the translation and he following me, as usual, in the Russian text. I had not read three sentences when he suddenly, to my complete surprise, dropped the manuscript and, looking up like a child proposing a new game, said:

"I have an idea. What do you say you and I together write a drama of the American Civil War!"

"Fine!" I said, trying to catch my breath.

"We would each bring something to it that the other lacks. You have a literary gift that I lack, and I could supply a factual knowledge of what a civil war is like!"

This man has the childlike charm of an artist. Perhaps my feeling of his weakness, of his being inadequate to his load, derives from the fact that his character as a man of action is the result of self-discipline and not of instinct. He has made out of himself something more, or at least other, than he is. I do not know. I merely record these two, or rather, three impressions: an utter absence of egotism, instinctive magnanimity, and something like weakness, as of a man overburdened with his own great strength.

It is unfortunate that I recorded the above impressions immediately, for now, after twelve days in Trotsky's home, my mood has changed to such an extent that I could hardly write them down. I feel "injured" by his total inward indifference to my opinions, my interests, my existence as an individual. There has been no meeting either of our minds or feelings. He has never asked me a question. He has answered all my questions, as a book would answer them, without interchange, without assuming the possibility of mutual growth. My pointed criticisms of his policy—that he has not thought out the implications of the problem of nationalities on a world scale, that he never should have let Stalin make "socialism in one country" the issue, thus jockeying him into the defense of a negative slogan—were met with mere lordly-hasty rejection. I was an amateurish creature needing to be informed of the technical truth which dwelt in his mind.

On the disputed question of Trotsky's "vanity," I still agree with Lunacharsky. His failing is subtler than that and more disastrous. He lives instinctively in a world in which other persons (except in the mass, or as classes) do not count. In youth he stood prodigiously high above his companions in brain, speech, and capacity for action, so that he never formed the habit of inquiring—he was always telling. His knowledge and true knowledge, his view and the right view, were identical. There is no bragging or vanity in this, no preoccupation with himself. Trotsky is preoccupied with ideas and the world, but they are his ideas and his view of the world. People, therefore, who do not adulate, go away from Trotsky feeling belittled. Either that, or they go away indignant, as I am.

Opinionated minds are usually far from wise; Trotsky is opinionated in the highest degree, but with wise opinions. Cranky people are usually old and barren of fruit. Trotsky is cranky, but young and fruitful.

I want to dwell on the manner in which his arrogance differs from vanity, or self-centered egotism. It is not a conscious thought, but an unconscious assumption that he knows, and that other people are to be judged and instructed. It is a postulate laid down in his childhood, as I said, and by his instincts. That, I now suspect, is why he is weak and indecisive and lacks judgment when frustrated. That is why he became almost hysterical when I parried with ease the crude clichés he employed to defend the notion of dialectic evolution. The idea of meeting my mind, of "talking it over" as with an equal, could not occur to him. He was lost. Similarly in the party crisis when the flood of slander overflowed him, he was lost. He never made one move after Stalin attacked him that was not, from the standpoint of diplomatic tactics, a blunder. Trotsky is much concerned with the task life imposes of making decisions. He told me once that in youth he passed through a period when he thought he was mentally sick, because he could never make up his mind about anything, but that as Commander of the Red Army he often astonished himself by the prompt assurance with which he gave orders to generals and colonels trained for a lifetime in military science.

It was in revolt against an inferior father's stubborn will that Trotsky developed the "excessive self-confidence" that Lenin warned against. What he needed, when that self-confidence cracked, was a father—an authority to defer to. That is what Lenin supplied. If you read Trotsky's History of the Russian Revolution carefully—as carefully as I, the translator, did—you will find that, although he praises others, he never attributes fundamental importance, either of initiative or judgment, to any Bolshevik but Lenin and himself. (That comes near, I must say, to being the objective truth about the October revolution, yet I think a diligent search might have discovered exceptions.)

Trotsky's idea of our collaborating on a play was, he confessed later, a scheme for making money. He is spending $1000 a month, according to his wife—his secretary tells me it is nearer $1500— keeping up the establishment he has founded here and in Berlin. There is, here in Prinkipo, besides the secretary and stenographers, a bodyguard of three proletarians, one continually on sentry duty at the door; there is another secretary in Berlin, an ingenious system for transporting books from the library there and getting them back on time. Besides that, Trotsky is supporting a sick daughter and her child in Prague. He does not live in luxury; there is practically no furniture in his villa; it is a barrack; and the food is simple to an extreme. He merely keeps up the habits of a War Minister after he has become the leader of a tiny proletarian party. His secretary, Jan Frankel, a Czechoslovak, confided to me his anxiety approaching despair because Trotsky, still living like a commissar, ignored completely the problem of financing his new party and his own gigantic labors. This was not a newly developed trait in Trotsky; he was always, even in his poverty-stricken days, incapable of hanging onto his earnings. Even the small change in his pocket would dribble away, thanks usually to some transparent form of *chantage,* in the course of a short walk down the street. In his present situation, however, it is a calamity, for it makes him overestimate the revolutionary integrity of certain dubious characters who chip in generously to the ever dwindling treasury of his "Fourth International." Money, of course, is beneath the contempt of a revolutionary idealist—gold, according to Lenin, was to be used for public urinals in the socialist society—but while we are on the way there it deserves a little steady attention.

The lack of comfort or beauty in Trotsky's house, the absence of any least attempt to cultivate the art of life in its perceptual aspect, seems almost despicable to me. A man and woman must be almost dead aesthetically to live in that bare barrack, which a very few dollars would convert into a charming home. The center of both floors of the house is a vast hall—not a hall exactly, but a room twenty feet long and fifteen feet wide with great double doors opening on a balcony which looks outward to the richly deep blue sea and downward to this bright red-cliffed island that crouches in the sea like a prehistoric animal drinking. In these vast rooms and on these balconies there is not an article of furniture—not even a chair! They are mere gangways, and the doors to the rooms on each side are closed. In each of these rooms someone has an office table or a bed, or both, and a chair to go with it. One of them, downstairs, very small and square and white-walled, with barely space for table and chairs is the dining room. The garden surrounding the villa is abandoned to weeds and these are running to seed. "To save money," Natalia Ivanovna explains. Through sheer indifference to beauty, I should say. Trotsky talks a good deal about art in his books and lays claim to a cultivated taste, but he shows no more interest in art than in that garden. I brought home one day from Istanbul photographs of the rarely beautiful sarcophagus of King Tobuit of Sidon that is in the Museum of Antiquities.

"Do you want to see one of the most beautiful works of sculpture in the world?" I said to Trotsky.

He grasped them hastily and handed them back to me almost with the same gesture. "Where were they found?"

"They were dug up in the ruins of Sidon."

"Who dug them up—Schliemann?"

I said, "No . . ." but by that time he was out of the door and on his way down to dinner.

His sole reaction had been, it seemed to me, to avail himself of the chance to reveal his acquaintance with the name of Schliemann. He had, at least, no interest whatever in the sculpture.

Although it is not so in his books, he seems in personal life to lack altogether the gift of appreciation. I think it is because no one ever feels appreciated by him that he fails so flatly as a political leader. He could no more build a party than a hen could build a house. With all his charming courtesy and fulfillment of every rule of good manners, including a sometimes quite surprising attentiveness to one's comfort, his social gift, his gift of friendship, is actually about on the level of a barnyard fowl. His followers, the followers of the great brain—the greatest political intelligence, I think, that we have today—make pilgrimages to him, and they come away, not warmed and kindled, but chilled and inhibited. Those of them, that is, who have individual will and judgment of their own. Hence he has no influence, properly so called. He does not sway strong people, but merely directs the weak.

Trotsky is playful and proud of being so, but I notice that his humor consists almost exclusively of banter. A perpetual poking of fun at the peculiarities of others, their nationality, their profession, their circumstances or tendencies—good-natured, smiling and charming, to be sure, but not varied with an occasional smile at himself, or any genial recognition of the funny plight of mankind in general.

And when you take part in the game, when you poke fun at him, he does not laugh, and his smile is never so cordial as when he, himself, lands a blow. I feel it is a little mean and picayune to make this hypercritical observation of Trotsky at play, for he can be delightful indeed, if you are firm enough on your own feet to accept his banter and give it back; but as a student of laughter—and of Trotsky—I can't refrain. To me it is all the more significant since it is a superficial trait.

As to his angularity, his cocksure terseness, that quality which led Lunacharsky to describe him as "prickly," I could not honestly be silent. It is a failure of instinctive regard for the pride of others, a lamentable trait in one whose own pride is so touchy. But he also disregards, when his own schemes are involved, the personal interests of others. And he is not forthright about it; he is devious even with his friends. As Trotsky's gift for alienating people has a certain historic importance, I am going to set down here the otherwise rather inconsequential details of an episode which alienated me.

I functioned for some time as a sort of unofficial literary agent for Trotsky in the United States. I got my pay in royalties in the end; I am not pretending to have been extravagantly generous; but I did, when he first arrived in exile, do quite a mountain of unpaid work for him. In the fall of 1931, however, he sent me an article to translate and sell for him, offering me twenty percent of what I got for it. He said he hoped for a large sum, as much, perhaps, as two hundred dollars. I translated it and took it to George Bye, a popular literary agent, who sold it to Liberty magazine for $1500. Of this George took ten percent for the sale and I, ten percent for the translation. This seemed not quite fair, and George, who was very generous, agreed in the case of future articles to let me have fifteen percent for the translation and take only five percent for the sale. This arrangement was reported to Trotsky; we sold two or three more of his articles, and he was delighted.

All went well until an article about Stalin arrived while I was absent on a lecture trip and the translation was delayed by a few weeks. During those weeks Trotsky, impelled by his book publishers to give an interview to the press, gave out the substance of the article. After that it could not be sold at a high price, but George persuaded the New York Times syndicate to pay a hundred dollars for it and give it the wide publicity that Trotsky, whatever the money payment, so much desired.

The delay, and the small fee, and his own costly mistake in giving out the interview, irritated Trotsky beyond measure. He decided to throw me over and deal directly with George Bye, trusting him to find a translator. I suspected this, because a long letter from George was lying on his desk the day I arrived in Prinkipo. I said nothing about it, but I noticed the next morning that the letter was gone. As he had never heard of George Bye, or had anything to do with him, except through me, this piqued my curiosity, and at the risk of impoliteness, I decided I would force him to be frank. To my seemingly casual question about the letter I had seen, he answered nervously: "Oh yes, when you told me you were going to Palestine and might not come to see me until afterward, I thought it might be best to get in touch with the agent directly."

I said: "It is all right for you to deal with George Bye directly, if you want to, but please remember that I have a contract with him giving me five percent of his commission, and if you deal directly with him without mentioning this, it will deprive me of a part of my earnings."

He was not impelled either by friendship, or by a recognition of my unpaid services to make any response to this. He was angry about that Stalin article. I was by this time heartily pleased with the prospect of not being interrupted every week or so with a too-long article to translate, but I ventured to remind him that George Bye did not have a Russian translator at his elbow. He merely said very sharply:

"No, it is absolutely impossible when you are traveling around Europe. The fate of that Stalin article showed me how impossible it is. I prefer to deal directly with a responsible agent."

My breath was taken by the harsh, irascible tone in which he said this. If I had been at home when the Stalin article came, and had translated and sold it immediately—say to Liberty—for a high price, it would have been in print and ready to publish when he gave away the substance of it to the press. The result would have been an explosion in the editorial rooms and a refusal to have anything to do with "Trotsky articles" in the future. I tried to say this, but he cut me off again sharply.

"No! Such delays are impossible. It is quite impossible to have the translator in one place and the agent in another."

In short, I was fired—and being in my heart glad of it, I took it in silence, and we changed the subject.

We both loved languages, and one of our pleasantest diversions was for him to dictate to me, in his horrendous English, answers to his American and British correspondents, which I would take home and bring back the next day polished off and typed on my portable machine. That same afternoon he drew out an illiterate inquiry from some woman in Ohio about her relatives in Russia, asking me if I knew who she was. When I answered, no, he said, "I guess there's no use answering." I agreed and crumpled the letter, or started to crumple and throw it in the wastebasket, but he stopped me with an outcry as though I were stepping on a baby's face.

"Is that the way you treat your correspondence? What kind of a man are you? That letter must be filed!"

I straightened the letter out, laughing at my mistake and passed it over to him, remarking, however, that it didn't seem to me very important to file a letter that wasn't worth answering.

There followed a certain amount of playful banter on that subject, and we went on with our fun, entirely friendly and good-natured.

The next day, however, I got to worrying, as everybody in the household did, about Trotsky's money problems. (In that respect, at least, he was a faithful follower of Karl Marx.) Realizing that if he sent articles to George Bye to be translated by anybody with a Russian accent who happened along, he would spoil his last chance of getting the needed $1500 monthly out of the American press, I ventured to raise again that question on which he had been so crisp. (Trotsky was a hero, you must remember, and moreover, he had been through such nerve-shattering experiences at the hands of the implacable avenger of excellence, Stalin, that no one could hold a grudge against him.)

"I feel a little embarrassed to resist you in this matter," I said, "because my own financial interests seem to be involved, but I can't help warning you that if you leave to a commercial agent the choice of a translator, you can easily lose in a month the position you've gained as a writer available to the American press. Of course, you can get statements on questions of the day published because you are Leon Trotsky, but that is a different thing from being a highly paid contributor to American magazines."

That was, at least, what I set out to say, but he interrupted me halfway through with an exclamation impatiently snapped out:

"No, no! I prefer not to send my articles to a man who grabs up his correspondence and throws it in the wastebasket!"

He imitated my gesture of the day before, but now without the slightest playfulness. He was still angry, I suppose, about the low price he got for that Stalin article. You would have to have in your memory, as I had, the painstaking drudgery of my two years' effort to protect his financial interests and teach him to get what was coming to him from the American press, to appreciate my indignation. Had he been anybody but Leon Trotsky, I would have given a red-hot expression to it and walked out.

Instead, I sat still until there came a brilliant inspiration. It was one of the few times in my life when I thought of the right thing to say.

"Lyef Davidovich, I can only answer you in the words of Lenin." And I quoted, in perfect Russian, from the famous testament: "Comrade Trotsky is apt to be too much carried away by the administrative aspect of things."

At this Trotsky relaxed and dropped back into his chair, laughing genially and completely, as though to say, "Touché!"

In a moment, however, he was forward and at it again, insisting now that I had been negligent about other articles—"the one on Hitler, for example." This was an article that, after several high-paying magazines refused it, George had finally sold to the Forum for three hundred dollars. There was nothing else to do with it and nobody was to blame.

At that point I gave up. Repeating once, and more insistently, my warning that a single article published prominently in a bad translation might ruin his chances, I added that I would let him know as soon as I was settled somewhere, and he might send me his articles or not, as he pleased. What he will do I have no idea, but that he will do anything out of consideration for my interests, or my legitimate stake in the enterprise, I regard as *ausgeschlossen*.

By "gave up," I mean that I abandoned the attempt at friendly conversation with Trotsky. I abandoned it about practical, as I had previously about theoretical, questions. I got away as quickly as I politely could, pleading the need to get back to the West in time to correct the proofs of the second volume of his history. To the end Trotsky kept insisting that we stay for several months at least, so that he and I might continue to "work together and go fishing." He was, so far as I could judge, blandly oblivious to the unwarmth and unfruitfulness of our relation.

The problem of Trotsky's character weaves so intricately in with the story both of the success and the failure of the Bolshevik revolution that it will never lose interest for historians. I hope a little light is cast on it by this memorandum, so immediately set down, of my visit to him after the story ended.

On my way home from Prinkipo, I met in Paris one of Trotsky's greatest admirers and closest friends—the closest, I think, after Christian Rakovsky—and we spoke of the subtle contradictions in Trotsky's character. To my hesitant and groping effort to say that he seemed to me to lack a feeling for others as individuals, his friend said shortly:

"*C'est tout-à fait vrai. Il n'a pas d'humanité. Elle lui manque absolument.*"

Notwithstanding this startlingly extreme confirmation of my impression, I feel that I left out of my memorandum something which, in justice to Trotsky, ought to have been included; a confession, namely, of my own failure of regard for the interests—indeed the most vital passions—of another. It was far from tactful of me to descend upon this intellectually lonely exile with a headful of fresh hot arguments against the religious belief by which he had guided his life to triumph and to this tragic end. It must have put him on edge against me. Perhaps that underlay some of the responses which I attributed to more trivial causes and to the general traits of his character. I find in our subsequent correspondence a letter in which, as though to heal an unmentioned wound, he took pains to mention that he had sent a certain manuscript direct to George Bye only because he had been given to understand that I was away from home.

I think Trotsky earnestly wanted to be regardful of the interests of others, but except in small matters and in the case of his wife, toward whom the most exquisite consideration seemed to be instinctive, he did not know how to do it. He lacked the gift of mutuality. He could apprehend, and discuss at times with keen penetration, the currents of emotion prevailing in other people, but he could not flow with them in a warm common stream.

CHARLES CORNELL WITH TROTSKY IN MEXICO [2]

One must understand Trotsky's passionate devotion to the cause of the oppressed to appreciate the full import of his work. He hated the injustices and indignities forced on man with his whole

---

[2] Charles Cornell, "With Trotsky in Mexico," in *Leon Trotsky The Man and His Work* (New York: Merit Publishers, 1969), pp. 64–67. Reprinted by permission of Pathfinder Press.

being. His polemics against political opponents are not at all the brilliant stylistic exercises which his petty-bourgeois critics make them out to be. Nor did he dash them off with the literary glibness which they attribute to him. Trotsky's powerful and incisive writing merely reflects his ardent convictions in the struggle for the liberation of mankind. The barbs of his sharp pen were completely at one with his hatred of all that degraded humanity. The style was truly the man. He did not write with facility at all; his polished writing was the result of strenuous and lengthy application.

Although the Old Man considered himself a slow writer, his literary output was prodigious. A shelf five feet long could be filled with his published works prior to 1918 alone. The secretary who was with him in Prinkipo relates that he finished the three volumes of the History of the Russian Revolution in thirteen months. His writings testify not only to the extraordinary fertility of his brain, but to his remarkable self-discipline.

Knowing that his time was limited, that Stalin's order for his death would be executed before he had contributed all he could in the task of preparing the Fourth International, Trotsky worked indefatigably. It was a race against time in which he spared nothing of his tremendous energy.

As was characteristic of him in all things, he sought for preciseness of expression and scientific exactitude in his writing. After the Russian stenographer had transcribed his first draft L.D.[3] would make corrections and revisions, cutting and pasting the manuscript until it was a long and continuous sheet. Part or all of the work was often revised and re-typed several times, before he was satisfied with the final draft.

This preciseness was apparent in everything he did, even in his relaxation. Making the most of conditions imposed upon him by necessity, he had taken up the hobby of raising chickens and rabbits, since they could be kept in the restricted area of the high-walled yard. The chore of caring for them he performed, too, with method and precision. The feed was prepared according to the most scientific formula he could obtain. The amount of food was carefully measured. He inspected the animals regularly for any signs of sickness or parasites. The chicken yards and pens were kept scrupulously clean. It was obvious that he enjoyed this diversion from his sedentary tasks.

L.D., a master of self-discipline, bent every minute of his time to

---

[3] Trotsky's given name and patronymic Lev Davidovich.

his will. Not a moment was wasted. He arose early, at about six in the morning, performed the chores in the yard, returned to his study and worked until breakfast. After breakfast he dictated letters and went on with his writing. Shortly before the noon meal he again took care of the animals. Unless some particularly urgent piece of work pressed for attention, he rested for an hour after lunch in accordance with the doctor's instructions. Sometimes at three in the afternoon a visitor would come and L.D. would spend an hour or so with him. Longer visits were infrequent, for his time was too limited.

Having fed and tended the chickens and rabbits in the evening he returned either to his study or, if dinner were ready, directly to the dining room. Dinner was usually a lively meal during which L.D. engaged everyone in conversation and joked with members of the household.

On many such occasions he would relate some occurrence or anecdote. I recall one following the May attack.[4] Col. Salazar, head of the Mexican secret police, had brought two of us back from jail, where they had tried to exact "confessions" of complicity in the assault from us. L.D. was, naturally, angry and indignant. Col. Salazar, L.D. told us, had tried to apologize and explain the act by saying that they had "only tried to uncover every possibility, to unravel every thread." L.D. replied to the Colonel, "But this time, Colonel, you happened to have a thread fastened to my coat!"

Most of his time was spent within the structure L.D. often referred to as "the jail"; the routine of the day being repeated monotonously. On occasion, but less frequently as reports of a GPU concentration in Mexico reached us, he went on "picnics." These were actually expeditions to gather cactus for L.D.'s collection. He especially admired this odd Mexican plant and as was typical of him, aspired to make his collection as nearly complete in its many varieties as possible.

He never undertook anything half-heartedly and his cactus collecting was no exception. On one occasion we accompanied some friends to Tamazunchale, a distance of about 380 kilometres from Coyoacan, in hopes of finding a special variety of cactus. We were unsuccessful, but on the way down L.D. had noticed some "viznagas" nearer to Mexico City. He decided, despite the fact that we reached the spot long after dark, to stop and collect a carful. It was a balmy

[4] On May 24, 1940 a group of gunmen staged a machine-gun assault on the Coyoacan headquarters. Trotsky narrowly escaped death.

night; L.D. was in a cheerful mood; he moved briskly about the little group digging cactus by the light from the headlamps of the cars.

This wholeheartedness permeated his entire activity. It was visible in his soldierly bearing, in his lively stride, in his punctuality. Whether it was a meal, a trip or a meeting, he insisted that it begin on time. I recall a conference held in his study with some friends from New York at which some of the guards came in late. After the first one arrived, L.D. got up and locked the door, putting the key in his pocket. Each time one of the latecomers knocked at the door L.D. arose from his chair, walked to the door and let the guard in. It was a most effective demonstration.

Before granting Trotsky permission to enter the country, Cardenas had requested that Trotsky pledge himself not to intervene in internal Mexican politics. Trotsky agreed to this stipulation and strictly adhered to it, to the last. Many reactionary elements, both in the United States and Mexico manufactured out of whole cloth lies attempting to prove Trotsky's close relations with Cardenas. Numerous absurd and utterly false articles appeared in Catholic organs stating that Cardenas never made a move without first consulting the "Red Demon of Coyoacan." The intent of such articles was to create the impression that the country was racing towards "atheism" and "bolshevik" revolution.

Trotsky did indeed hold Cardenas high in his appreciation, because of all the "democratic" politicians in the world who espoused the right of asylum for political exiles, Cardenas was the only one who lived up to the principle. However, Trotsky neither saw Cardenas nor anyone representing him, nor did he communicate with him except in matters pertaining to the security of the household.

Remaining true to his promise not to intervene in the political life of Mexico did not, however, prevent Trotsky from following systematically and carefully the political developments in the country. One might say Mexico was no exception, for he followed the news of every country with avid interest. Conversations with friends, artists, intellectuals, workers and *campesinos*—with people from the varied social categories he encountered—supplemented and rounded out the news he gleaned from the press and gave him a profoundly intimate understanding of Mexican life.

His knowledge of Mexico and his sympathy for the struggle of the workers and *campesinos* against the imperialists and *hacendados* made it possible for him to engage a worker around the house in an intimate conversation or to discuss land reforms in the simplest terms with the *campesino* he met on a walk.

He believed that a revolutionist was characterized by his attitude towards colonial people and their struggle for freedom.

Any expression of chauvinism, any reflection, no matter how veiled, of the typical bourgeois attitude towards colonial people aroused L.D.'s anger and brought down wrath on the head of the offender. One striking example of this sensitivity occurs to me. A letter was once received from a petty-bourgeois radical who was at the time a member of the Socialist Workers Party. This comrade, by the way, considered himself an authority on colonial problems. In the letter a comrade's inability to visit the Old Man was explained as resulting from a delay at the border "due to typical Mexican stupidity." Trotsky read the letter, underlined the phrase in blue and placed large red exclamation marks in the margin. He gave it to me with the statement that I should reply to this characterization of the Mexicans as being monstrously false and flowing from an arrogant Yankee imperialist attitude!

TROTSKY IN HISTORY

12
In the Judgment of Historians

The polemical battle concerning Trotsky's role in history has done more to obscure than to illuminate the question. His defenders and opponents have done everything possible to present him as either the personification of modern Marxist thought or the Judas of the socialist cause. Only in the late 50s did the first serious attempts to evaluate Trotsky's role in history appear.

The first selection (by the professional historians) is taken from Edward Hallett Carr's magisterial History of the Bolshevik Revolution. *Carr is regarded as one of the foremost English specialists on Soviet Russia. When the first volumes of his* History *appeared at the height of the Cold War, it is interesting to note that he was criticized by both Soviet and Western historians. That early criticism, no doubt, reflected the olympian detachment that Carr was capable of exercising in his work. In the form of a miniature portrait Carr presents his reader with a vivid picture of Trotsky's life and the nature of his triumphs and failure.*

The second excerpt is from Isaac Deutscher's monumental biography of Trotsky, which friendly critics have suggested will perhaps be recognized as the greatest biography of our century. In this selection Deutscher attempts both an explanation and evaluation of Trotsky's place in Russian history immediately before his expulsion from the Soviet Union in 1929.

EDWARD HALLETT CARR [1]

Lev Davidovich Trotsky (original name Bronstein) was born in 1879 at the village of Yanovka in the Ukraine, his father belonging to the not very numerous class of Jewish independent small farmers. At the age of nine he was sent to school in Odessa, living with relatives of his mother. His last year of schooling—1896–1897 —was passed at Nikolaev, where he first began to read forbidden books and became politically conscious. Early in 1897 he joined a revolutionary group engaged in underground political work, and underwent conversion to Marxism. In the following year he was arrested, spent the next two years in a succession of prisons, and was sent to Siberia in 1900. In 1902 he made his escape and, travelling via Vienna, Zurich and Paris, joined Lenin and Martov in London. His literary talents, marked by a certain flamboyance of style, had already won him the party nickname of Pero or Pen: he quickly became a contributor to *Iskra,* earning the admiration of Lenin and the jealous disapproval of Plekhanov.

The second party congress of 1903 was an important turning-point in Trotsky's career. Differing from Lenin on the character of the party organization, he came down on the side of Martov and the Mensheviks. In the following year, in a pamphlet entitled *Our Political Tasks* and published under Menshevik auspices, he pronounced himself in favour of "opportunism in the organizational question" as against Lenin's "organizational rigorism," and made a bitter and sweeping personal attack on Lenin, whom he denounced as a "Maximilian Robespierre" and a "slipshod attorney," and accused of a desire to establish a "dictatorship over the proletariat." He soon broke with the Mensheviks, fell under the influence of Parvus, a German Social-Democrat of Russian origin, who inspired his theory of "permanent revolution," and returned to Russia to participate actively in the 1905 revolution, becoming, at the age of twenty-six, the last president of the short-lived Petersburg Soviet, and demonstrating his capacity to sway and dominate an audience of workers. After a public trial which enhanced his reputation in revolutionary circles he spent another short period in Siberia, but escaped in time to attend the fifth party congress in London in 1907. From this time till 1917 he consistently attempted to occupy a

[1] From E. H. Carr, *Socialism in One Country* (New York: The Macmillan Company, 1958) I, 139–52. Copyright © 1959 by Edward Hallett Carr. Reprinted by permission of The Macmillan Company of New York and of Canada, and Macmillan London and Basingstoke.

position "outside the factions," struggling to reconcile Bolsheviks and Mensheviks in the name of a "general party" line. Trotsky's view of the nature of the coming revolution was now far nearer to that of the Bolsheviks than of the Mensheviks. But, whereas Menshevism was always fluid and open to compromise, Bolshevism had hardened under Lenin's hand into a rigid core of doctrine which tolerated no dissent and treated as enemies those who rejected any item of it; and this meant in practice that Trotsky found himself far more often at loggerheads with the Bolsheviks, and with Lenin in particular, than with the Mensheviks. The fact that Lenin and Trotsky were at this time, in their different styles, already the two outstanding figures in the Russian Social-Democratic movement, and that there was no Menshevik of comparable stature to draw Trotsky's fire, merely deepened and sharpened the differences between them.

The years from 1907 to 1914 furnished that rich literature of controversy and mutual recrimination between the rival leaders which afterwards helped to build up the tradition of a fundamental incompatibility between the doctrine of Lenin and the doctrine of Trotsky. It was at this period that differences of opinion between them about "permanent revolution" and the role of the peasant, which, as the sequel showed, were never more than differences of emphasis, became inflated in the heat of controversy into differences of principle; and this period also produced the abundant literature of mutual vituperation which played so conspicuous a role in later controversies. The outbreak of war in 1914 brought about no immediate mitigation of the antipathy between them. Trotsky passed two years of the war in Paris, where in conjunction with Martov he edited a Russian anti-war newspaper *Nashe Slovo,* to which Lunacharsky, Ryazanov, Lozovsky, Chicherin, Radek and Rakovsky were regular or occasional contributors. Trotsky now stood on the extereme Left of the party. His views on the war differed in form rather than in substance from those of Lenin. But his eclecticism and willingness to cooperate with Mensheviks still estranged him from the Bolsheviks; and his stern internationalism made him unsympathetic to the compromise which Lenin was prepared to make with the principle of national self-determination. At the end of 1916 Trotsky was expelled from France, and spent the first three months of 1917 in New York. He at once became a member of a Left-wing group in which Bukharin and Kollontai were leading figures and a contributor to the journal of the group, *Novyi Mir.*

He evidently offended Kollontai, who wrote to Lenin that "Trotsky's arrival strengthened the Right wing at our meetings" and had delayed the endorsement of the Zimmerwald programme; and this letter provoked the last of those personal outbursts of Lenin against Trotsky ("What a swine that Trotsky is!") which were afterwards so freely exploited by Trotsky's enemies. On the outbreak of the February revolution he left for Russia, and, after a long detention by the British naval authorities at Halifax, Nova Scotia, finally reached Petrograd in May 1917. Lenin met him at first "with a certain restraint and hesitation." But, from the moment when Trotsky decided to join the Bolshevik party and to accept its organization and discipline, the difficulties melted away. In the critical months of 1917 Trotsky consistently saw eye to eye with Lenin: at this time there was, as Lenin recorded, "no better Bolshevik." Trotsky's experience and prestige as leader of the Petrograd Soviet of 1905 were invaluable, and he played the largest single part in organizing the *coup* of October 1917. Its brilliant success, and Trotsky's subsequent work in the recruitment and organization of the Red Army, made him in the eyes of the world the equal partner of Lenin: the names "Lenin and Trotsky" were coupled wherever the Russian revolution was spoken of. In the party the role of Lenin's principal lieutenant could not be denied him. It was true that Trotsky continued to have differences with Lenin in this period—on Brest-Litovsk, on the advance to Warsaw, on the relations of trade unions to the state, to name only the most famous. But it was also fair to recall the occasions on which he had stood with Lenin against other party leaders—in opposition to a coalition in November 1917, in support of the employment of "specialists" in the Red Army, in defence of the monopoly of foreign trade, in opposition to the coercion of Georgia in 1921–1922. Such alternations of agreement and disagreement were perfectly possible at this period between loyal party members. Lenin's criticism, in the testament, of Trotsky's "too far-reaching self-confidence" and "disposition to be too much attracted by the purely administrative side of affairs" was balanced by the recognition of him as "personally . . . the most able man in the present central committee," and implied no grain of doubt of his loyalty and devotion.

The position of Trotsky in the party was challenged only when Lenin was incapacitated and when Trotsky's rivals came together to block his potential claim to the succession. He himself remarked that "the beginning of the struggle with 'Trotskyism' coincides with the end of Lenin," though he failed to understand the reason. When Lenin disappeared from the scene, it quickly became patent how much of the strength of Trotsky's position had been due to Lenin's active support. While he had a following in the rank and file of the party, the other party leaders were his implacable enemies. What now brought about his downfall was hostility not to his policies, but to his person. It would be nearer the truth to say that, between 1924 and 1927, Trotsky's policies were discredited because he propounded them than that he was discredited for propounding unacceptable policies. He made mistakes; but mistakes which would have been lived down and forgotten if committed by others proved fatal to him. It was his record, his outlook, his personality which were the real target of attack and the real causes of his defeat. An examination of these will throw an indirect but significant light on the history of the period.

Of all the Bolshevik leaders Trotsky was the most western and the least specifically Russian. Born in a Jewish family well above the poverty line and with some intellectual ambitions, in a part of Russia where anti-Semitism was rife in the period in which he grew up, educated in a school which was a German foundation, and where half the pupils in his day were still German, he can hardly have escaped some perhaps unconscious prejudice against things Russian. By way of contrast, he conceived "an idealization of the foreign world, of western Europe and America," whither millions of his compatriots, including a high proportion of Jews, were to migrate in the two decades before 1914. He himself came to western Europe at the impressionable age of twenty-three—a refugee from the Russian police. But, above all, the Russia against which Trotsky reacted was the peasant Russia of his youth. The mature Trotsky was wholly urban. The town was the symbol of everything progressive: "the history of capitalism," he had written in 1906, "is the history of the subordination of the country to the town." Every Russian Marxist believed in the economic superiority of western capitalist society and in the backwardness of the primitive peasant Russian economy: every Russian Marxist reacted against the Slavophil myth. But Trotsky showed particular zest in dwelling on the nullity of the Russian contribution to civilization. In statesmanship Russia had "not got beyond third-rate imitations of the Duke of Alba, Colbert, Turgot, Metternich or Bismarck." In philosophy and social science, what Russia had given to the world was "nothing, a round zero." Even Trotsky's admiration of the classics of Russian

literature had a European flavour; Karataev in *War and Peace,*
he remarked, was "the least comprehensible, or at any rate the most
remote from the European reader," of Tolstoy's characters. The
whole conception of the revolution was for Trotsky inseparable from
that of the impact of European civilization on backward Russia:

> The revolution means the final break of the people with Asianism,
> with the 17th century, with holy Russia, with ikons and cockroaches,
> not a return to the pre-Petrine period, but on the contrary an as-
> similation of the whole people to civilization.

To seek salvation in the west was Russia's revolutionary destiny.
In April 1916 Trotsky still deprecated "the national revolutionary
messianic mood which prompts one to see one's own nation-state
as destined to lead mankind to socialism."

The distinctively western cast of Trotsky's thought helps to explain why before 1914 he found himself more at home with the
more westernized Mensheviks than with the Bolsheviks. But he was
also, of all Russian social-democrats, the only one who, during this
period, achieved easy personal relations with the social-democrats of
western Europe. The association with Parvus gave him his first
entry into German party circles. Between 1907 and 1914 his position
outside the two Russian factions made him the best interpreter of
Russian party affairs to western European socialists, who shared his
impatience of the doctrinal niceties of Russian party strife. In Berlin
he was an assiduous visitor to the house of Kautsky, where he met
the other German party leaders including the veteran Bebel; and
he was the only Russian whose contributions were welcomed by
Vorwärts and *Neue Zeit.* In Vienna he was on friendly terms with
the Austrian socialist leaders. He developed at this time a keen interest in the art, literature and intellectual movements of the west.
Through Joffe, who was psychoanalysed by Adler, he had at any
rate a superficial acquaintance with the work of Freud. In Paris in
1915 and 1916 he came to know the French leaders of the extreme
Left. After the foundation of Comintern he long remained, on the
strength of these personal contacts, the main authority on relations
with the French party. In the Russian party he made himself the
champion of such supposedly western virtues as orderliness and
punctuality. If Trotsky struck Lunacharsky in 1905 as "unusually
elegant, unlike the rest of us," if visitors to Moscow in the days of
his greatness often noticed the "elegance" of his dress, and an

American admirer described him as "highly bourgeois," this was another way of saying that Trotsky preferred European conventions, affecting neither Lenin's proletarian cloth cap nor Stalin's Russian blouse. To describe Trotsky as the most European, and Stalin as the least European, of the early Bolshevik leaders is to state one of the underlying causes of the incompatibility between them. In the party where, after Lenin's death, men with little or no experience of the west were gradually coming to the top, the western quality of Trotsky's chosen ways account for the ready support which he at first obtained in most of the western communist parties, in the Russian party it was quickly turned against him. The resolution of the party central committee of January 1925 which passed judgment on him described Trotskyism as "a falsification of communism in the spirit of approximation to 'European' patterns of pseudo-Marxism, i.e., in the last resort, in the spirit of 'European' social democracy."

Another quality put Trotsky at the opposite pole to Stalin. Of the original Bolsheviks only Stalin, and perhaps Zinoviev, were not pre-eminently intellectuals; the rest (and the same was true of nearly all the Mensheviks) were men of ideas, men who resorted naturally to the written word and would have been uneasy about any course of action which could not be justified by theoretical argument. But in this respect Trotsky towered above them all. For sheer force of intellect nobody in the party was a match for him. His anticipation of the dangers of personal dictatorship in the party in his pamphlet of 1904; his analysis of the future course of the revolution in *Results and Prospects* in 1906; his diagnosis of the different, but characteristic, chinks in the ideological armour of both Mensheviks and Bolsheviks in the article of 1909—all these were extraordinary examples of penetrating acumen. The more testing conditions of political responsibility after 1917 revealed no falling off in intellectual power, though they brought out some of the defects of this quality in practical politics. The debate over Brest-Litovsk found Trotsky in the familiar posture of attempting to build a platform mid-way between two conflicting groups. The "no war, no peace" formula was a brilliant and ingenious improvisation. Its application was a gamble which nearly succeeded. But the verdict may be that to gamble in such a situation is not a mark of the highest statesmanship. In the succeeding years, Trotsky was, on a remarkable number of occasions, the first to elaborate and put forward policies which were eventually adopted, sometimes after he had been denounced for defending

them. He was, so far as the record goes, the first advocate of NEP—
at any rate in the party—a year before its acceptance. He was the
protagonist of industrialization and planning at a time when these
were denounced by the party leadership as destructive of NEP and
of the "link" with the peasantry. The maintenance of labour armies
and the "statization" of the trade unions, which were vehemently
rejected when he proposed them, were realized, in substance though
not in form, several years later. But this sequence of miscarriages—
or of successes out of due time—suggests Trotsky's fundamental
weakness as a responsible politician. He had an unfaltering, at
times almost uncanny, perception of the social and economic trends
of his time, and of the policies which would one day be demanded
to take account of them. But he did not possess that supreme political sense of tact and of timing which is given to the great masters of
statecraft. Once he had diagnosed the need for action, he lacked
the patience to wait till the moment was ripe. The capacity to manipulate men, and to shape situations, in the interest of the course
which he judged necessary eluded him. He had much of the common failing of the intellectual in politics: intolerance of the crude
realities of the exercise of political power.

It was Trotsky's position in the party as the outstanding westerner
and as the outstanding intellectual which, more than any specific
issue of doctrine or policy, differentiated him from Lenin. Lunacharsky summed up the difference in the acute and provocative
verdict that Trotsky was a more orthodox Marxist than Lenin. If
Marxism is regarded primarily as a rigid analysis of the contradictions of the capitalist system and of bourgeois society, and only
secondarily as a programme of action, if its economic and so-called
"determinist" elements are exalted above its political and voluntarist
aspects, then Trotsky was the better Marxist; and this interpretation of Marxism, which can be supported by many passages of Marx
himself, is on the whole the one which has prevailed in the west.
But this was not the interpretation which, under the leadership of
Lenin, prevailed in the Bolshevik revolution. Lenin brought to the
interpretation of Marx's teaching a flexibility and an adaptability
which were foreign to Trotsky's attitude, but which are probably
essential to any application of theory to practice. Both Lenin and
Trotsky liked to invoke history. But, while Lenin was fully alive to
the necessity of moulding the course of history to his programme,
Trotsky tended to treat history as an objective reality which was
accessible to intellectual analysis, and was bound to justify that

analysis in action if the analysis were correct. The masses, by their spontaneous action, were the executors of the laws of history: the essence of the Bolshevik revolution was "the forcible entrance of the masses into the realm of rulership over their own destiny." From this court there was no appeal. Trotsky relegated his defeated opponents to the dustbin of history. But, in so doing, he deprived himself of any real answer when, in the hour of his own defeat, he found himself consigned to the same destination. His autobiography and many of his subsequent writings revolved round the tormenting question why he was defeated, why the masses failed to rise to his support—questions which for him could be answered only in terms of some error of analysis. He patently failed to answer them, either to his own satisfaction or to that of the reader. It is significant that in the concluding sentences of his autobiography he sought "consolation" in a quotation not from Marx, but from his old enemy Proudhon—not in an analysis of history, but in a gesture of defiance to it.

The singularities of Trotsky's political destiny were closely interwoven with those of his personal character. The quality which Lenin called "self-confidence" and others bluntly branded as arrogance isolated him among his equals. An acquaintance of his early years, in a hostile but perceptive sketch, wrote of the desire "to rise above all, to be everywhere and always first" as the "fundamental quality" of his character; and this gave his revolutionary convictions an austere and almost inhuman note which distinguished them from the equally intense but emotionally warmer convictions of Lenin:

> The revolution and his active "ego" coincided. Everything that was outside his "ego", and therefore did not interest him, did not exist for him.
>
> The workers interested him as necessary instruments of his activity, of his revolutionary work; his comrades interested him as a means with the cooperation of which he exercised his revolutionary activity. He loved the workers, he loved his comrades in the organization, because in them he loved himself.

Between 1903 and 1917 he continued to play a lone hand; and, when in 1917 the logic of the revolution and the magic of Lenin's personality made him a Bolshevik, they did not bring his isolation to an end. There was more than a grain of truth in Kamenev's later taunt that Trotsky "entered our party as an individualist, who thought, and still thinks, that in the fundamental question of the revolution it is not the party, but he, comrade Trotsky, who is right." For Trotsky, even the Marxist sense of history seemed to take on a personal colour, and to centre round his own role on the historical stage. Unlike Lenin, wrote Lunacharsky, who "never looks at himself, never glances into the mirror of history, never even thinks of what posterity will say of him," Trotsky "looks at himself often," "treasures his historical role," and coveted "the halo of a genuine revolutionary leader."

After Trotsky's downfall many who had once praised and flattered hastened to denigrate and condemn. But there is contemporary evidence of the ambivalent attitude of the other leaders towards him and of their resentment of his authority and prestige: indeed, nothing else could explain the rapidity and ease with which the coalition was formed against him when Lenin withdrew from the scene. "More feared than loved, perhaps—that is possible," wrote a French communist whose record of a visit to Moscow in 1921 appeared with a preface by Trotsky, "but his ascendancy is prodigious." "I love Trotsky, but am afraid of him," wrote the poetaster Demyan Bedny a little later. Angelica Balabanov, an unsympathetic critic, passed a harsher judgment:

> His arrogance equals his gifts and capacities, and his manner of exercising it in personal relations creates very often a distance between himself and those about him which excludes both personal warmth and any feeling of sympathy and reciprocity.

Lunacharsky referred to Trotsky's "nonchalant, high and mighty way of speaking to all and sundry," and noted that "a tremendous imperiousness and a kind of inability or unwillingness to be at all amiable and attentive to people" condemned him to "a certain loneliness" in the party: he had "practically no immediate supporters." A specialist without party affiliations who saw a good deal of the leaders at this time acutely observed Trotsky's isolation:

> In any gathering of these old Bolsheviks Trotsky remained an alien. . . . Trotsky compelled them to respect him, to pay heed to every word he spoke. Yet they resented it bitterly, or at least were dissatisfied and jealous whenever Lenin saw fit to defer publicly to Trotsky.

It was easy for Lenin, the uncontested leader, to overlook Trotsky's sudden and rapid promotion and to forget his past record in admiration of his present deserts. It was more difficult for those jealous old Bolsheviks who felt that an intruder had supplanted them both in authority and in Lenin's favour. Trotsky never seems to have realized the handicaps imposed on him by his late accession to the party. His behaviour accentuated them. His outstanding services to the party, and Lenin's ungrudging recognition of them, were a sufficient passport to pre-eminence; he sought no other. He saw no reason to conciliate his enemies and rivals, and heedlessly added to their number.

It was doubtless this human shortcoming which Lenin had in mind when he wrote in the testament of Trotsky's addiction to "the purely administrative side of affairs." His capacity as an administrator was second only to his intellectual power. The effortless success of the October *coup* of 1917 owed much to his organizing genius; the creation of the Red Army was his supreme achievement; and any department administered or supervised by Trotsky was a model of efficiency. Nor did this exhaust the astonishing range of his gifts. He was probably the greatest orator of the revolution. Before a limited and informed party assembly, his studied rhetorical effects were less effective than Lenin's direct simplicity; and Stalin underlined the point when he missed the "simple and human" touch in Trotsky's exposition of Leninism. But Trotsky's occasional flamboyance did not, like that of Zinoviev, mask an intellectual void or a weakness of inner conviction. It sprang from a fierce, uncontrollable passion; and in the ability to move a mass audience by the passionate sweep of his eloquence Trotsky stood out above any of his contemporaries. Yet the great intellectual, the great administrator, the great orator lacked one quality essential—at any rate in the conditions of the Russian revolution—to the great political leader. Trotsky could fire masses of men to acclaim and follow him. But he had no talent for leadership among equals. He could not establish his authority among colleagues by the modest arts of persuasion or by sympathetic attention to the views of men of lesser intellectual calibre than himself. He did not suffer fools, and he was accused of being unable to brook rivals. Where Lenin was supreme, Trotsky failed altogether.

Thus the political climate of the period, combined with his own weaknesses of character, sealed Trotsky's doom. Self-confident, haughty and aloof among his colleagues, secure in his own superiority and unconscious or contemptuous of the ruffled emotions of those who felt themselves overshadowed by him, he felt no need to defend himself against the powerful forces accumulated against him. Referring to the first attacks of the other leaders upon him in the winter of 1923–1924, he nonchalantly boasted that he had not read "any of these things." He made no attempt, till it was far too late, either to organize his friends or to divide his enemies. Trotsky had no political instinct in the narrower sense, no feeling for a situation, no sensitive touch for the levers of power. It was this defect which rendered him blind, in the years before the revolution, to the significance of Lenin's insistence on rigorous organization, and which, after the revolution, made him politically no match either for Lenin, whom he outshone in many spheres, or for Stalin, whom he eclipsed in almost all. But, even more than these personal short-comings, the evolution of events contributed to his defeat. As an intellectual he lost his foothold in a time when theory was beginning to be at a discount, when political life revolved round the empirical solution of current practical problems, and the balance between conflicting factions and interests was maintained by clever political maneuvring. As a wholehearted and impenitent westerner, he was out of place in a period when a return to Russian national tradition was being cunningly blended with the achievements of the revolution. As a revolutionary to the finger-tips, he was an incongruous figure in an age which seemed (though falsely seemed) to be set on a path of consolidation and stabilization. As an individualist, whose past recalcitrance to party discipline was unforgotten and unforgiven, he was suspect in a party which hymned the praises of collective leadership and was obsessed by the bogy of a Bonaparte. Trotsky was a hero of the revolution. He fell when the heroic age was over.

ISAAC DEUTSCHER [2]

The helplessness and dumbness of the peasantry were part and parcel of the political lethargy of the post-revolutionary society at large; and this formed the background to the extra-ordinary activity and seeming omnipotence of the ruling bureaucracy. Trotsky repeatedly grappled with this aspect of the situation; and repeatedly his mind ran away from it. Krupskaya once made the remark, which in all probability she had picked up from Lenin, that Trotsky was

[2] From Isaac Deutscher, *The Prophet Unarmed, Trotsky: 1921–1929* (London: Oxford University Press, 1959), pp. 461–68. Copyright © 1959 by Oxford University Press. Reprinted by permission of the publisher.

inclined to underrate the apathy of the masses. In this Trotsky was true to himself and his character as a revolutionary. The revolutionary is in his element when society is in action, when it unfolds all its energies, and when all social classes pursue their aspirations with the maximum of vigour and *élan*. Then his perception is at its most sensitive, his understanding at its acutest, and his eye at its quickest and sharpest. But let society be overcome by torpor and let its various classes fall into a coma, and the great revolutionary theorist, be he Trotsky or even Marx, loses something of his vision and penetration. This condition of society is most uncongenial to him and he cannot intellectually accommodate himself to it. Hence Trotsky's errors of judgement. Even when he made the utmost allowance for the post-revolutionary weariness of the masses he still shrank from fathoming its full depth. Thinking ahead, he still envisaged all social classes and groups—kulaks as well as workers and army leaders as well as the various Bolshevik groupings—in action and motion, in a state of self-reliance and animation, ready to jump at one another and to fight their titanic battles. His thought was baffled at the sight of Titans drowsy and indolent whom a bureaucracy could tame and tie hand and foot.

Because ultimately he identified the process of revolution with the social awareness and activity of the toiling masses, the evident absence of that awareness and activity led him to conclude that, with Stalinism victorious, 'the film of the revolution was running backwards,' and that Stalin's part in it was that of Kerensky in reverse. Here again the fallacy is obvious; but the core of truth in it should not be overlooked. The film was not running as the precursors and the makers of the revolution had expected: it was moving partly in a different direction—but not backwards. Stalin's role in it was not that of Kerensky in reverse. The film is still on; and it may still be too early to pass final judgement on it. In theory it may yet be possible for it to end in a setback for the revolution as grave as that which earlier great revolutions, the French and the English, had suffered. But this possibility appears to be extremely remote. When Trotsky wrote that the film was running backwards he meant that it was moving towards the restoration of capitalism. Actually it moved towards planned economy, industrial expansion, and mass education; and these, despite all bureaucratic distortion and debasement, Trotsky himself recognized to be essential prerequisites for socialism, the *sine qua non* for the ultimate fulfilment of the revolution's promise. The prerequisites were admittedly not the fulfilment; and the Soviet Union of the 1950's had enough reasons to look back upon the record of Stalinism, or at least upon some of its facets, with sorely disillusioned eyes. But it did not see the triumphant kulak and N.E.P.-man at the end of Stalin's road.

Was Stalin's record one of Bonapartism? Trotsky did not use the term in the accepted meaning as signifying merely 'government by the sword' and personal rule. The wider Marxist definition of Bonapartism is that of a dictatorship exercised by the state machine or the bureaucracy at large, of which military autocracy is only one particular form. What, in the Marxist view, is essential to Bonapartism is that the State or the Executive should acquire *political* independence of all social classes and establish its absolute supremacy over society. In this sense Stalin's rule had, of course, much in common with Bonapartism. Yet, the equation offers only a very general and vague clue to the understanding of the phenomenon in all its complexity and contradictoriness. Stalin exercised his rule not so much through an 'independent' state machine as through the 'independent' party machine through which he also controlled the state. The difference was of great consequence to the course of the revolution and the political climate of the Soviet Union. The party machine considered itself to be the only authorized guardian and interpreter of the Bolshevik idea and tradition. Its rule therefore meant that the Bolshevik idea and tradition remained, through all successive pragmatic and ecclesiastical re-formulations, the ruling idea and the dominant tradition of the Soviet Union. This was possible only because the idea and the tradition were firmly anchored in the social structure of the Soviet Union, primarily in the nationalized urban economy. If any partial parallel to this state of affairs were to be drawn from the French Revolution, it would have to be an imaginary one: we would have to imagine what revolutionary France would have looked like if the Thermidorians had never overthrown Robespierre, and if he had ruled France, in the name of a crippled and docile Jacobin party, throughout all those years that the historian now describes as the eras of the Directory, the Consulate, and the Empire—in a word, what France would have looked like if no Napoleon had ever come to the fore and if the revolution had run its full course under the banner of Jacobinism.

We have seen that the rule of the party machine had in fact been initiated at the close of the Lenin era. It had been inherent in the dominance of the single party which Lenin himself saw as being essentially the dominance of the Bolshevik Old Guard. Lenin's government in his last years might therefore be described, in accordance with Trotsky's use of the term, as 'Bonapartist,' although it lacked the feature which formed the true consummation of Bonapartism, namely, personal rule. Thus, when in 1928 Trotsky spoke about the danger of Bonapartism he saw a phase of development which had been largely accomplished many years earlier as still looming ahead. Since Lenin's day the despotism of the party machine had, of course, become increasingly aggressive and brutal. But the specific content of the stormy political history of these years, from 1921 till 1929, consisted not merely and not so much in this as in the transformation of the rule of a single party into the rule of a single faction. This was the only form in which the political monopoly of Bolshevism could survive and become consolidated. In the opening pages of this volume we found the single-party system to be a contradiction in terms. The various Bolshevik factions, groups, and schools of thought formed something like a shadowy multi-party system within the single party. The logic of the single-party system implicitly required that they be eliminated. Stalin spoke with the voice of that logic when he declared that the Bolshevik party must be monolithic or it would not be Bolshevik. (Up to a point, of course, the party ceased to be Bolshevik as it was becoming monolithic.)

The logic of the single-party system might not have asserted itself as strongly as it did, it might never have become as ruthless as it was and its implication might never have become explicit, or the system might even have been undone by the growth of a workers' democracy, if the whole history of the Soviet Union, encircled and isolated in its age-old poverty and backwardness, had not been an almost uninterrupted sequence of calamities, emergencies, and crises threatening the nation's very existence. Almost every emergency and crisis posed all major issues of national policy on the knife's edge, set the Bolshevik factions and groupings at loggerheads, and gave to their struggles that indescribable vehemence and intensity which led to the substitution of the rule of a single faction for that of the single party. At the point our narrative has reached, in the show-down between the Stalinists and the Bukharinists, this process was coming to a close. What still lay ahead was the quasi-Bonapartist consummation: the substitution, in the early 1930's, of the rule of the single leader for that of a single faction. It was this consummation —Stalin's autocracy—that Trotsky clearly foreshadowed, however he erred in other respects.

Even now, however, Trotsky did not perceive the ascendancy of Stalinism as an inevitable result of the Bolshevik monopoly of power. On the contrary, he saw it as the virtual end of Bolshevik government. Thus, while Stalin presented the undivided rule of his own faction as the consequence and final affirmation of the rule of the single party, Trotsky viewed it as a negation. In truth, the Bolshevik monopoly of power, as established by Lenin and Trotsky, found in Stalin's monopoly both its affirmation and its negation; and each of the two antagonists now dwelt on a different aspect of the problem. We have traced the transitions through which the rule of the single party had become the rule of the single faction and through which Leninism had given place to Stalinism. We have seen that the things that had been implicit in the opening phase of this evolution became explicit and found an extreme or exaggerated expression in the closing phase. To this extent Stalin dealt in realities when he claimed that in his conduct of party affairs he followed the line set by Lenin. But Trotsky's emphatic denial of this was no less strongly based on realities. The rule of the single faction was indeed an abuse as well as a consequence of the rule of the single party. Trotsky, and following him one Bolshevik leader after another, protested that when they had, under Lenin, established the Bolshevik political monopoly they had sought to combine it with a workers' democracy; and that, far from imposing any monolithic discipline on the party itself, they had taken the party's inner freedom for granted and had indeed guaranteed it. Only the blind and the deaf could be unaware of the contrast between Stalinism and Leninism. The contrast showed itself in the field of ideas and in the moral and intellectual climate of Bolshevism even more strongly than in matters of organization and discipline. Here indeed the film of revolution ran backwards, at least in the sense that Stalinism represented an amalgamation of Marxism with all that was primitive and archaically semi-Asiatic in Russia: with the illiteracy and barbarism of the muzhik on the one hand, and the absolutist traditions of the old ruling groups on the other. Against this Trotsky stood for undiluted classical Marxism, in all its intellectual and moral strength and also in all its political weakness—a weakness which resulted from its own incompatibility with Russian backwardness and from the failures of socialism in the West. In banishing Trotsky, Stalin banished classical Marxism from Russia.

Yet, such were the paradoxical fortunes of the two antagonists, that just when Trotsky was being ejected from his country Stalin set out to uproot, in his own barbaric manner, that Russian back-wardness and barbarism which has as if regurgitated classical Marx-ism, and the Stalinist bureaucracy was about to put into effect Trotsky's programme of primitive socialist accumulation. Trotsky was the authentic inspirer and prompter of the second revolution of which Stalin was to be the practical manager in the coming decade. It would be futile to speculate how Trotsky might have directed that revolution, whether he would have succeeded in car-rying out Russia's industrialization at a comparable pace and scale without condemning the mass of the Soviet people to the privation, misery, and oppression they suffered under Stalin, or whether he would have been able to bring the muzhik by persuasion to col-lective farming rather than to coerce him into it. These questions cannot be answered; and the historian has more than enough work in analysing events and situations as they were, without trying to ponder events and situations that might have been. As things were, the political evolution of the 1920's predetermined the manner in which Russia's social transformation was to be accomplished in the 1930's. That evolution led to autocracy and monolithic discipline and consequently to *forcible* industrialization and collectivization. The political instruments that would be needed for primitive so-cialist accumulation had been forged throughout the 1920's; and they were now ready for use. They had been forged not in any de-liberate and conscious preparation for the task ahead but rather in the unpremeditated course of the inner-party struggles by which the Bolshevik monopoly of power had become the Stalinist mo-nopoly. However, if autocracy and monolithic discipline formed, as the Marxist would say, the political superstructure of primitive socialist accumulation, they also derived from this a measure of self-justification. Stalin's adherents could argue that without autocracy and monolithic discipline that accumulation, on the scale on which he carried it out, could not be undertaken. To put it plainly, from the long contests of the Bolshevik factions there had emerged Sta-lin's 'firm leadership' for which he may have striven for its own sake. Once he wielded it, he employed it to industrialize the Soviet Union, to collectivize farming, and to transform the whole outlook of the nation; and then he pointed to the use he was making of his 'firm leadership' in order to vindicate it.

Trotsky repudiated Stalin's self-vindicatory claims. He continued to denounce his adversary as a Bonapartist usurper. He was to acknowledge the 'positive and progressive' aspects of Stalin's second revolution and to see them as the realization of parts of his own programme. He had, we remember, already compared his and the Opposition's fate with that of the Communards of Paris, who although they failed to conquer as proletarian revolutionaries in 1871 had nevertheless barred the way to a monarchist restoration. This had been their victory in defeat. The great transformation of the Soviet Union in the 1930's was Trotsky's victory in defeat. But the Communards had not been reconciled to the Third Republic, the bourgeois republic which might never have prevailed without them. They remained its enemies. Similarly, Trotsky was for ever to remain unreconciled to the *bureaucratic* second revolution; and against it he was to call for the self-assertion of the working classes in a workers' state and for freedom of thought in socialism. In doing this he was condemned to political solitude, because all too many of his closest associates allowed themselves, partly from frustration and weariness and partly from conviction, to be captivated or bribed by Stalin's second revolution. The Opposition in exile was on the point of virtual self-liquidation.

Was Trotsky then in conflict with his time? Was he fighting a hopeless battle 'against history'? Nietzsche tells us:

> If you want a biography, do not look for one with the legend: 'Mr. So-and-So and his times', but for one in which the title page might be inscribed 'A fighter against his time'. . . . Were history nothing more than an 'all embracing system of passion and error' man would have to read it as Goethe wished *Werther* to be read— just as if its moral were 'Be a man and follow me *not!*' But, fortunately, history also keeps alive for us the memory of the great 'fighters against history', that is against the blind power of the actual . . . and it glorifies the true historical nature in men who troubled themselves very little about the 'Thus It Is', in order that they might follow a 'Thus It Must Be' with greater joy and greater pride. Not to drag their generation to the grave, but to found a new one—that is the motive that ever drives them onwards. . . .

These are excellent words despite their underlying subjectivist romanticism. Trotsky was indeed a 'fighter against his time,' though not in the Nietzschean sense. As a Marxist he was greatly concerned with the 'Thus It Is' and was aware that the 'Thus It Must Be' is the child of the 'Thus It Is'. But he refused to bow to 'the blind power of the actual' and to surrender the 'Thus It Must Be' to the 'Thus It Is.'

He fought against his time not as the Quixote or the Nietzschean Superman does but as the pioneers do—not in the name of the past but in that of the future. To be sure, as we scrutinize the face of any great pioneer we may detect in it a quixotic trait; but the pioneer is not a Quixote or a Utopian. Very few men in history have been in such triumphant harmony with their time as Trotsky was in 1917 and after; and so it was not because of any inherent estrangement from the realities of his generation that he then came into conflict with his time. The precursor's character and temperament led him into it. He had, in 1905, been the forerunner of 1917 and of the Soviets; he had been second to none as the leader of the Soviets in 1917; he had been the prompter of planned economy and industrialization since the early 1920's; and he was to remain the great, though not unerring harbinger of some future reawakening of the revolutionary peoples (—to that political reawakening the urge to transcend Stalinism which took hold of the Soviet Union in the years 1953–6 was an important pointer; still faint yet sure). He fought 'against history' in the name of history itself; and against its accomplished facts, which all too often were facts of oppression, he held out the better, the liberating accomplishments of which one day it would be capable.

13

Current Soviet Views of Trotsky and the Trotskyist Movement

Trotsky's role in the Bolshevik Revolution has been largely erased by Soviet historians. What remains of the story has been purposely twisted, so that there is little resemblance between his actual career and the version known to Soviet citizens. The following article is a good example of contemporary Soviet treatment of Trotsky and the movement which bears his name to the present. Again, Trotsky and his present-day followers are seen as a lurking force of evil threatening to sabotage the working-class movement throughout the world. The second excerpt is taken from the Bol'shaia Sovetskaia Entsiklopediia, *the Soviet equivalent of the* Encyclopaedia Britannica.

A. BASMANOV [1]

The activities of the Trotskyites in the capitalist countries never seem to flag. Their efforts to influence the youth, their constant intrigues, are doing serious damage to the revolutionary struggle. In addition, they proliferate fabricated propaganda materials, which the bourgeois press then quickly accepts and publicizes.

Just what does contemporary Trotskyism stand for?

Flotsam of a Wrecked Ship

Rodney Arismendi, First Secretary of the Central Committee of the Communist Party of Uruguay, describes the groups that sometimes call themselves Trotskyite parties as the flotsam of a long-wrecked ship. The simile fits rather aptly. For Trotsky's whole apparatus was so totally wrecked four decades ago that the organiza-

[1] From A. Basmanov, "Trotskyism in the Modern World." From *Communist Viewpoint*, vol. 2, no. 3 (May–June 1970), 39–42. Reprinted by permission of Progress Books, Canada.

tions of its followers are indeed like the fragments of a sunken ship.

The ideological and organizational defeat of Trotsky himself in our country has gone down in the history of the Communist movement as a remarkable example of principled, uncompromising struggle against opportunism. Our Leninist Party not only preserved the purity of its ranks, it enriched communism the world over with its invaluable experience of exposing ultra-Leftism and its essentially capitulationist nature. Since then, true to Lenin's behests, other Communist Parties have fought the Trotskyites' attempts to disrupt and destroy the international working-class movement from within.

Expelled in the nineteen-twenties and thirties from Communist and Workers' Parties, the Trotskyites soon began making strenuous efforts to find new forms of anti-Communist struggle. In some countries they formed small groups which, being outside the organized working-class movement, continued their subversive activities from without, smuggling their concepts and views into the workers' parties.

With the political adventurism typical of him, Trotsky decided to knock together an international organization out of these fragments. This he hoped to oppose to the Communist International. A handful of his followers from several European countries, gathering in Paris in 1930, declared themselves to be "the international Left-wing opposition." Somewhat later, this "opposition" announced eleven conditions for admission to its ranks. These included a denial of the very possibility of victory of socialism in a single country, denunciation of the economic policy of the U.S.S.R., and recognition of the "theory of permanent revolution."

Soon the Trotskyites found out, however, that it was much easier to work out conditions for admission than to extend their ranks, even insignificantly. When they faced worker audiences, they met with sharp rebuffs. At the same time, the internal dissensions tearing their organizations apart grew from bad to worse.

It was on such shaky foundations that Trotsky nonetheless decided to build his "International." What's more, before it even began to be formed, he already started acting, in 1934–37, on behalf of a non-existent "Soviet section" of the non-existent "International."

In 1938, Trotsky was finally able to gather a group of his followers for a "constituent conference" in Paris. This conference, attended by only twenty-one participants, stated that both the "international Left-wing opposition" and its bureau "have in the past shown an inability to act." Nevertheless it decided on the founding of the "Fourth International."

The slogans advanced at the time by Trotskyism further exposed it as a political trend hostile to the working class. Its program was based on a negative attitude toward everything that Communists and the international working-class movement as a whole fought for. The Trotskyites fiercely attacked the very idea and practice of establishing a united anti-fascist front. They also denied the necessity for a struggle for peace, since, they alleged, war was the mother of revolution. The hypocrisy of their pseudo-revolutionary theories was already clear from their whole policy of that period. From dark predictions about the destruction of the Soviet Union in case of imperialist aggression (Trotsky wrote: ". . . The defeat of the Soviet Union is inevitable. From the technical, economic and military points of view, imperialism is incomparably stronger. Unless it is paralyzed by revolution in the West, imperialism will sweep out of existence the system born of the October Revolution.") the Trotskyites passed in the years of World War II to openly subversive activity in the anti-fascist movement.

Measuring with the same yardstick the policy of the fascist bloc countries and the countries subjected to aggression, they denied the liberating nature of the struggle waged by the forces opposed to fascism, and even after Hitler's attack on the Soviet Union, declared, as late as the end of 1941, that "the very concept of anti-fascist struggle" was "a Communist fraud and invention." The Trotskyites broadcast their fabrications about the creation of the anti-Hitler coalition being an act hostile to the interests of both the Russian and the world revolution. They also called for preventing the opening of the Second Front showing themselves up in their true colors —enemies of socialism and allies of the forces of reaction and fascism. They discredited themselves so thoroughly that by the end of the war their groupings in a number of countries simply disintegrated.

With the strengthening of socialism's position in the post-war period, internecine strife and disagreements in the Trotskyite camp became even more widespread, and differences began to appear between its two main groupings, each of which defended its own platform of anti-Communist activities. One of these, out of tactical consideration, advocated certain departures from the old Trotskyite formulations as well as revisions of some of Trotsky's own views. The other, on the contrary, demanded that all the old principles be kept intact. In 1953, the "Fourth International" split into the so-called "International Committee" and the "International Secretariat." Later on, still another grouping—the "Latin American Bureau"—branched out separately. Even the Trotskyites themselves were compelled to admit at the time that their already feeble "International" was going through such a serious crisis it could hardly hope to find a way out.

Since the beginning of the nineteen-sixties, the Trotskyite groups and groupings, with their one foot in the grave, have again been trying to raise their heads. Seeing in Mao Tse-tung's policy a fresh opportunity to revive anti-Communist activity, they hastened to snatch at it, at the same time shouting about the "vitality" and "correctness" of their ideas. The Trotskyite congress held in 1961 stated in a special resolution that the differences that had arisen in the Communist movement "open up before Trotskyism such opportunities for action as have never existed before."

The attempt to overcome the split was made by the American Trotskyites, who, in their message circulated in 1968, declared that the position of the Mao Tse-tung group "determines an important stage of reconstruction" of the "Fourth International." The message, which called for unity in the name of struggle against the Communist Parties, was the core of the debate at the so-called unity congress held in the summer of 1963.

In actual fact, however, no unification was achieved. The "Latin American Bureau" and part of the British, French, and Japanese Trotskyites refused to take part in the congress. The remaining few participants divided into a "majority" and a "minority," which to this day remain at loggerheads.

Present-day, just as pre-war, Trotskyism represents a medley of groups and groupings to be found in some West European countries, the United States, Canada, a number of Latin American countries, in Japan, Ceylon, and in Australia. The number of members in each of these groups does not as a rule exceed several dozen. In some cases they constitute microscopic "initiative" groups which, however, each publish a paper or a magazine.

How, then, do the Trotskyite groups manage to keep their heads above water? What do they hope to accomplish? First of all, they capitalize on the fact that considerable social strata tending toward the ultra-Left have in recent years been drawn into the anti-imperialist movement and the struggle against the monopolies. They bank on the petty bourgeois, who is being ruined and is suffering privations and who, as Lenin indicated, "easily goes to revolutionary extremes but is incapable of perseverance, organization, discipline, or steadfastness."

Intellectuals and students are sometimes also infected with Leftism. Representatives of these strata are often inclined to deny the leading role of the working class in the anti-monopolist struggle. They even try to subordinate the working-class movement to themselves, to infect it with petty-bourgeois illusions.

Trotskyism does possess a certain tenacity because its ultra-Left views accord with the sentiments of sections of petty-bourgeois intellectuals, of declassed elements, and various adventurers. Trotskyism does adapt itself to such sentiments. Besides, the experience of class struggle shows that Leftism often comes as a reaction to the "original sin" of Right-wing social democracy, rejecting revolutionary forms of class struggle. The leaders of Trotskyism themselves do not conceal the fact that they hope to find their support among the extremist petty-bourgeois elements. And the latter, who as a rule are ready to denounce capitalism in words, are at the same time inclined to reduce all forms and methods of struggle against capitalism to adventurism alone.

Here and there the Trotskyites operate in the same environment as the groupings of Mao Tse-tung's supporters. During last year's student actions in France, for instance, the Trotskyites and the Maoists actively helped each other, inciting the youth with equal zeal to rashness and violence. The Trotskyites' alliance with pro-Maoist organizations is also to be observed in some of the Latin American countries.

The "body of theory" of contemporary Trotskyism shows up its complete ideological impotence, its inability to offer positive solutions to the major problems of revolutionary struggle. The fact that it produced no clear, definite program after the war speaks for itself. The numerous statements made by the various "congresses" cannot even be called a substitute for such a program, for they are full of contradictory, hastily proposed and as hastily rejected theories. Trotsky's theory of permanent revolution, long since discredited, remains the fig leaf hiding the ideological nakedness of his followers.

BOL'SHAIA SOVETSKAIA ENTSIKLOPEDIIA [2]

Trotskyism: A form of Menshevism, this political tendency is named after that irreconcilable enemy of Leninism, L. D. Trotsky.

As early as the Second Congress of the R.S.D.R.P. (i.e. Russian Social Democratic Labor Party) (1903) Trotsky opposed the revolutionary policies enunciated by V. I. Lenin. He joined the Mensheviks at the Congress in defending Martov's formula for the first paragraph of the R.S.D.R.P. Statutes. In so doing Trotsky was opposing the organization of a new type of powerful, militant, and disciplined Marxist party. On the question of the Party's program, Trotsky took a stand against the dictatorship of the proletariat.

During the first Russian Revolution of 1905–1907, Trotsky again sided with the Mensheviks. He opposed Lenin's ideas of the proletariat's commanding role in the revolution, as well as of the necessity and possibility of uniting the workers and peasants. Dismissing the peasantry as a reactionary class, Trotsky advanced the demagogic slogan of "No Tsar, and a Workers' Government." Rejecting Lenin's theory of the development of a bourgeois-democratic revolution into a socialist one, Trotsky and his supporters defended their own, anti-Marxist theory, known as that of "permanent revolution."

Throughout the years of the Stolypin reaction, V. I. Lenin led the Bolsheviks in a struggle to maintain Marxist principles within the Party. This was waged on two fronts: against the Liquidators and against the Otzovists. Trotsky, on the other hand, supported the Menshevik-Liquidators, the Bundists, and the other enemies of Leninism. Unmasking Trotsky's hypocrisy, Lenin, in 1914 . . . named him "the Judas Trotsky."

In 1912 Trotsky brought the Liquidators, the Otzovists, and the Trotskyites together in the "anti-Party August bloc," which was directed against both V. I. Lenin and the Bolshevik party. But the Liquidationist policy of the Trotskyites was disguised as Centrism, or an attempt at reconciliation. They maintained that they stood apart from both the Bolsheviks and the Mensheviks, and were struggling to make peace between the two groups.

During the First World War, the Trotskyites attacked Lenin's policies on all the basic questions of war, peace, and revolution,

---

[2] "Trotskyism," from Bol'shaia Sovetskaia Entsiklopediia, 2nd ed. (Moscow, 1956): XLIII, 301–2. Trans. by David R. Jones.

but again hid their own opportunism under "Leftist" phrases. They were, in fact, against the defeat of "their own" bourgeoisie in the imperialism war, and against turning this struggle into a civil war. The Trotskyites were Social-Chauvinists and Centrists in disguise. They opposed V. I. Lenin's theory of socialism revolution, that maintained that even if power was at first seized in only a handful [of] (or even one) capitalist countr[ies], it was possible for socialism to triumph. And this the Trotskyites derided as an example of "national narrow-mindedness."

In August, 1917, the Trotskyites, as members of the "interdistrict" group, joined the Bolshevik Party. At this time the "interdistrict" people declared that they agreed with the Bolsheviks on every issue and so requested membership in the Party. But it was later revealed that the Trotskyites had attempted to spread, in the ranks of the working class and of its Party, disbelief with regard to the strength of the socialist revolution, the creating of an alliance between the workers and peasants, and the possibility of a socialist transformation in the Soviet land. In 1918 the Trotskyites opposed the conclusion of the Brest peace with the Germans, and in 1920 they adopted an anti-Leninist position on the question of the role of the professional unions.

Again, in 1923, the Trotskyites opposed the Leninist policy in the peasant question and rejected the union of the proletariat and the peasantry. The Thirteenth Party Conference and the Thirteenth Congress of the R.K.P. (B.), [i.e. Russian Communist Party (Bolshevik)] (1924), the Fourteenth Party Conference and the Fourteenth Congress of the V.K.P. (B.) [i.e. All-Russian Communist Party (Bolshevik)] (1925), condemned the platform of the Trotskyite opposition. This was denounced as a petty-bourgeois deviation from Marxism and a revision of Leninism. The Trotskyite attacks on the Party's Leninist policies for the building of socialism in the U.S.S.R. were suppressed.

In 1926 the Trotskyite-Zinoviest anti-Party bloc was formed. The Party had already fought with Trotskyism, as a political trend, in the pre-October period and again in 1918, after the Soviet power had been established. At this time the Party set out first of all to bury Trotskyism as an ideological force, and then to destroy its organizational framework.

The Fifteenth Congress of the V.K.P. (B.) (1927) declared that participation in the Trotskyite opposition and the propagandizing of its views was incompatible with membership in the Bolshevik

Party. The Congress approved the resolution of the Central Committee and the Central Committee of the Comintern on the expulsion from the Party of Trotsky and Zinoviev. It was also resolved to expel all those who had been active in the Trotskyist-Zinoviest bloc. In 1929, Trotsky was exiled from the U.S.S.R. for his underground, anti-Soviet activities.

The Struggle of foreign Communist and Workers' parties against Trotskyism is considered to be one of their most important tasks.

14
The Trotsky Debate Continued

*The decade of the sixties saw the polemical argu-
ments concerning Trotsky's ideas reach a positive and fruitful
level of discussion. The old campaign of vilification between
Stalinists and Trotskyists was replaced among western Marxists
by a far more searching and objective attempt to re-examine
the case. In order to illustrate the continuing debate between
Marxists, two arguments are presented which attempt to explain a particularly important aspect of Trotsky's contribution
to political theory—"permanent revolution."*

NICOLAS KRASSÓ [1]

Socialism in One Country Versus Permanent Revolution

The dispute over this issue dominated the ideological debates
of the twenties. Lenin had established what was undoubtedly a
correct position at the time of Brest-Litovsk. He said that the Bolsheviks should always be thinking of varying possibilities, not of
false certainties. It was naive to speculate whether revolutions
would or would not occur in the West, in general. Bolshevik strategy should not be based on the presumption of an occurrence of a
European revolution; but neither should the possibility of one be
discarded. After Lenin's death, however, this dialectical position
disintegrated into polarized opposites within the party. Stalin effectively wrote off the possibility of international revolutions, and
made the construction of socialism in one country the exclusive task
—both necessary and possible—of the Bolshevik party. Trotsky
declared that the October Revolution was doomed unless international revolutions came to its aid, and predicted that these revolutions were certain to occur. The falsification of Lenin's position
is evident in either case.

[1] From Nicolas Krassó, ed. *Trotsky: The Great Debate Renewed* (St. Louis,
Missouri: New Critics Press, Inc., 1972), pp. 31–35. Reprinted by permission of
New Left Review, Ltd., London.

It may be argued that Stalin, by discounting the possibility of successful European revolutions, effectively contributed to their eventual defeat—this accusation has often been made against his policies toward Germany and Spain. There was, indeed, an element of the self-fulfilling prediction in socialism in one country. However, given this criticism—which is precisely that Stalin's policies represented a debasement of Lenin's strategy—the superiority of Stalin's perspective over Trotsky's is undeniable. It forms the whole historical-practical context in which the struggle for power discussed above unfolded. No matter how strong Stalin's position in the apparatus, it would have availed him little if his basic strategic line had been invalidated by the course of political events. It was, on the contrary, confirmed by history. In this lay Stalin's ultimate, unshakable strength in the twenties.

Trotsky's Conception. What was Trotsky's strategic conception, by contrast? What did he mean by "permanent revolution"? In his brochure of 1928 of that name, he included three quite separate notions in the same formula: the immediate continuity between democratic and socialist stages of the revolution in any given country; the permanent transformation of the socialist revolution itself, once victorious; and the inevitable linkage of the fate of the revolution in any one country with that of the world revolution everywhere. The first was to imply a generalization of his view of the October Revolution, discussed above, now proclaimed a law in all colonial countries. The second was banal and uncontroversial—no one was going to deny that the Soviet state would ceaselessly undergo change. The critical notion was the third one: the position that the survival of the Soviet revolution depended on the victory of revolutions abroad. Trotsky's arguments for this assertion, the crux on which the whole of his political position rested, are astonishingly weak. He provides, in effect, only two reasons why socialism in one country was not practicable. Both are vague in the extreme. They seem to be that Russia's entry into the world economy would render her hopelessly vulnerable to capitalist economic blockade and subversion. "The harsh curbings of the world market" are invoked, without any account of what precise impact they would have on the nascent Soviet state. Secondly, Trotsky appears to argue that the U.S.S.R. was militarily indefensible, and would collapse to external invasion unless European revolutions came to its help. It is perfectly evident that neither of these arguments was justified at the time, and that both were indeed disconfirmed by actual event.

Soviet foreign trade was a motor of economic development, not of regression and capitulation—a factor of progress in the rapid accumulation of the twenties and the thirties. Nor did the world bourgeoisie pounce upon the Soviet Union in unison, sending supranational armies marching on Moscow. On the contrary, intercapitalist contradictions were such that they delayed imperialist attack on the U.S.S.R. for twenty years after the Civil War. When Germany eventually invaded Russia, the Soviet state, industrialized and armed under Stalin and assisted by bourgeois allies, was able to throw the aggressors back triumphantly. There was thus no substance in Trotsky's thesis that socialism in one country was doomed to annihilation.

Theoretical Error

What is important to isolate here is the basic theoretical error that underlay the whole notion of permanent revolution. Trotsky, once again, proceeded from a schema of (hypostatized) mass social forces—bourgeoisie versus proletariat in alliance with the poor peasantry—in one country, to a universalization of this equation via its direct transposition onto a world scale, where the "international" bourgeoisie confronted the "international" proletariat. The simple formula "permanent revolution" effected this enormous jump. All it omitted was the *political* institution of the *nation*—that is to say, the whole formal structure of international relations and the system it constitutes. A "mere" political institution, bourgeois at that, evaporated like so much phosphorescence before a monumental class confrontation dictated inexorably by sociological laws. The refusal to respect the autonomy of the political level, which had previously produced an idealism of class action innocent of any party organization, now produced a global *Gleichschaltung*—a planetary social structure, soaring above its articulations in any concrete international system. The intermediary level party or nation —is in both cases simply omitted.

This idealism has nothing to do with Marxism. The notion of permanent revolution had no authentic content. It was an ideological concept designed to unify disparate problems within a single compass, at the cost of an accurate account of any of them. The expectation that successful revolutions were imminent in Europe was the voluntarist consequence of this monism. Trotsky failed to understand the fundamental differences between Russian and Western European social structures. For him, capitalism was one and indivisible, and the agenda of revolution was one and indivisible, either side of the Vistula. This formal internationalism (reminiscent of that of Luxemburg) in fact abolished the concrete international differences between the various European countries. Stalin's instinctive mistrust of the Western European proletariat, and his reliance on Russian particularism, showed a more accurate, if narrow and uncritical, awareness of the segmented nature of Europe in the twenties. Events vindicated his belief in the enduring importance of the nation as the unit demarcating one social structure from another. Political agendas were not interchangeable across geographical frontiers in the Europe of Versailles. History kept different times in Paris, Rome, London, or Moscow.

ERNEST MANDEL [2]

We now reach the third tier of Krassó's critique of Trotsky's Marxism, in a certain sense the decisive one, and obviously the weakest link in his chain of reasoning: his critique of Trotsky's "expectations" of international victories of the revolution after 1923.

This whole part of Krassó's essay is dominated by a strange paradox. Krassó started out by accusing Trotsky of underestimating the role of the party. But Trotsky's hope of successful revolutions in the West, Krassó now states, was based upon his failure "to understand the fundamental differences between Russian and Western European social structures." In other words, *objective conditions* made world revolution impossible, at least between the two world wars. In opposition to Trotsky's alleged "voluntarism," Krassó here defends a position of crude socioeconomic determinism: as revolutions have not won (yet) in the West, this proves that they could not have been victorious, and if they could not have been victorious it was because of the "specific social structure" of the West. The role of the party, of the vanguard, of the leadership, the "autonomy of political institutions," is now completely eliminated from the picture—by Krassó himself, and in polemics *against* Trotsky. A strange somersault indeed. . . .

But what about Lenin? How does Krassó account for the fact that Lenin, who, to quote Krassó, "theorized the necessary relationship between party and society," was as fervently convinced as Trotsky of the necessity of building communist parties and a Communist International? Does Krassó consider this "futile voluntarism" on

Lenin's behalf? How does he explain the fact that, years after Brest-Litovsk (Krassó here commits a historical distortion by earlier insinuating the contrary), Lenin continued to think that an international extension of the revolution to the West and the East was unavoidable?

Krassó can only try and construct a difference between Lenin's and Trotsky's position on the dialectical interrelationship between the October Revolution and the international revolution, by attributing to Trotsky three mechanistic and childish ideas: the idea that revolutions were "imminent" in Europe; that capitalist conditions were everywhere, at least in Europe, equally ripe for revolution without any difference between specific nations; and that the victory of these revolutions was "certain." Needless to say, Krassó will find it impossible to substantiate any of these allegations. It is easy to find overwhelming documentary proof of the contrary.

As early as the Third Congress of the Comintern (1921), Trotsky, together with Lenin (both were "at the right wing" of that Congress), stated unmistakably that, after the first wave of postwar revolutionary struggles, capitalism had now gained a breathing spell in Europe. What was on the agenda was not "immediate revolution," but the preparation of the communist parties for *future* revolution, i.e., a correct policy to win the majority of the working class and create a cadre and leadership capable of leading these parties to victory when new revolutionary situations occurred. Criticizing Bukharin's and Stalin's Draft Program of the Communist International, Trotsky stated explicitly in 1928:

> The revolutionary character of the epoch is not that it permits the accomplishment of the revolution, that is, the seizure of power, at every given moment. Its revolutionary character consists in profound and sharp fluctuations and abrupt and frequent transitions from an immediately revolutionary situation, that is, such as enables the Communist Party to strive for power, to a victory of the fascist or semifascist counterrevolution, and from the latter to a provisional regime of the golden mean (the Left bloc, the inclusion of social democracy into the coalition, the passage of power to the party of MacDonald, and so forth), immediately thereafter forcing the antagonism to a crisis again and acutely raising the question of power.

In his final writings, he again and again characterizes our epoch as a swift succession of revolutions, counterrevolutions, and "temporary stabilizations," a succession which precisely creates the *ob-*

jective conditions for building a revolutionary vanguard party of the Lenin type.

Here indeed is the nub of the question, which Krassó does not even pose and obviously cannot answer for that reason. What is the basic assumption that is at the bottom of Lenin's organizational concepts? As Georg Lukács so aptly characterized it, it is the assumption of the *actuality of the revolution,* i.e., the conscious and deliberate preparation for conquest of power by the proletariat when revolutionary situations occur, and the profound conviction that, given the objective laws of motion of Russian society, such revolutionary situations *had* to occur sooner or later. When Lenin wrote his book on *Imperialism,* under the influence of Rudolph Hilferding's *Finanzkapital,* and when he drew up a balance sheet of the significance of World War I, he correctly extended the notion of actuality of the revolution to the entire imperialist world system: the weakest links would break first; but precisely because they were links of one chain, the entire chain would be broken up progressively. This was his justification for calling for the formation of a Third International. This was the programmatic foundation of the Comintern.

Now this is a central concept with which you cannot dally frivolously. Either it is theoretically correct and confirmed by history— and in that case not only is the "third law of permanent revolution" adequate, but the main responsibility for the working-class defeats of the twenties, thirties, and early forties can then be put squarely at the door of inadequate leadership. Or Lenin's central concept after August 4, 1914, was incorrect, and experience has shown that objective conditions were not ripe for the periodic arising of revolutionary situations in the rest of Europe—and in that case it is not only Trotsky's "third law of permanent revolution" that was a "theoretical error" (to quote Krassó), but all of Lenin's endeavors to build communist parties, organized with the purpose of leading the proletariat to the conquest of power, then stand condemned as criminal splitting. Is not this, after all, what social democrats have been claiming for more than fifty years, with the same basic argument about "sociopolitical conditions" in the West being "unripe" for revolution, and Lenin "failing to understand the fundamental differences between Russian and Western European social structures"?

The balance sheet can be drawn up very quickly, at least on the level of historical experiences. Leaving aside minor countries, there was a revolutionary situation in Germany in 1918–19, 1920, and in

1923, and a great possibility of turning a successful defense against the threat of Nazism into a new revolutionary situation in the early thirties; there was a revolutionary situation in Spain in 1931, 1934 and 1936–37; there was a revolutionary situation in Italy in 1920, in 1945, and in 1948 (at the moment of the attempted murder of Palmiro Togliatti); there was a revolutionary situation in France in 1936 and in 1944–47. Even in Britain, there was something called a general strike in the mid-twenties. Ample literature, including writings of noncommunist and nonrevolutionary sources, attests to the fact that in all these situations the unwillingness of the masses to tolerate the survival of the capitalist system, and their instinctive drive to take society's fate in their own hands, coincided with wide confusion, division, if not near-paralysis among the ruling classes —Lenin's definition of a classical revolutionary situation. If we extend the picture to the whole world, with the Chinese revolution of the twenties and the Vietnamese uprising of the early thirties blending at the end of World War II into two powerful revolutions that stimulated a worldwide revolutionary movement of the colonial and semicolonial countries, then, surely, the definition of this half-century as "the age of permanent revolution," which Isaac Deutscher and George Novack chose as the title for a paperback selection of Trotsky's writings, is an adequate summary of historical experience.

Krassó now comes to the most extraordinary statement of his essay: the defeats of the European revolution in the twenties, thirties, and early forties prove that "the superiority of Stalin's perspective over Trotsky's is undeniable." Because, you see, Trotsky foresaw victorious revolutions, while Stalin "discounted the possibility of successful European revolutions." But wasn't it precisely the opposite? Trotsky did not believe at all in automatically victorious revolutions—neither in Europe, nor anywhere else. He only tirelessly fought for a *correct policy* of the communist movement, which would enable it eventually—if not the first time, then the second, or the third one—to transform revolutionary situations into revolutionary victories. By advocating *incorrect policies,* Stalin contributed heavily to the defeats of these revolutions. He taught the Chinese Communists to put their trust in Chiang Kai-shek and, in a public speech held on the very eve of Chiang's wholesale massacre of the Shanghai workers, expressed his firm belief in the executioner as a "faithful ally." He taught the German Communists that social democracy was their main enemy, and that Hitler would either be unable to conquer power or would be unable to stay in power more than a few months: they would be the real victors very soon. He taught the Spanish Communists to stop their revolution and to "first win the war," in alliance with the "liberal" bourgeoisie. He taught the French and Italian Communists to build a "new democracy" that would not be any more "entirely" bourgeois because of a few communist cabinet ministers and a few nationalizations.

All these policies ended in disaster. Yet when Krassó draws up the balance sheet of the disasters, he concludes . . . that Stalin's perspective was undeniably (!) superior to Trotsky's, for, you see, he "discounted the possibilities of successful European revolutions"! Perhaps the Stalin course of the Third International, the transformation of the Comintern from a tool of world revolution into a simple aid to diplomatic maneuvers of the Soviet government, and the theory of achieving the building of socialism in a single country, had something to do with the absence of successful European revolutions? Or would Krassó go so far as to impute to Stalin the intention of deliberately organizing these defeats . . . just to "prove" the "superiority" of his perspectives over those of Trotsky?

As Marxists, we have to pose a final question. Stalin's "mistakes" in the realm of the Communist International cannot be explained away as accidental results of his "lack of understanding" or "Russian provincialism," any more than the disastrous results of his policies inside the Soviet Union can be explained by the thoroughly un-Marxist formula of the "personality cult." [3] His "mistaken" tactics in no way corresponded to the interests of the Soviet or the international proletariat. They cost millions of deaths which could have been saved, decades of avoidable sacrifices, and years of terrible sufferings under the iron rule of Fascism. How, then, can one explain the fact that Stalin systematically opposed or sabotaged all attempts by communist parties to take power, outside of the realm

---

[3] But wasn't Stalin's policy vindicated by the U.S.S.R.'s victory in World War II, ask many people, and as Krassó also insinuates? To see things like this—completely passing over in silence the tremendous price paid for that victory, and the innumerable avoidable victims and defeats (including during the war: a whole literature has sprung up on the Soviet Union around this theme!) is to present a distorted picture of reality. A man on the fifth floor refuses to take the elevator or even to switch on the light, but wants perforce to descend a narrow staircase in the dark. He slips, as could be expected, falls down the stairs, but thanks to his robust constitution does not break his neck, but only both arms and legs, and is even able to walk on crutches again after four years. This is obviously proof of a strong constitution; but does it argue against taking the elevator?

of the Soviet army, anywhere in the world, for nearly thirty years? [4] Surely, a *social* explanation must be found for this astonishing fact. Such a systematic policy can only be explained as the expression of the *particular interests of a special social grouping* inside the Soviet society: the Soviet bureaucracy.

This grouping is not a new class. It does not play a particular and objectively necessary role in the process of production. It is a privileged outgrowth of the proletariat after its conquest of power under objective conditions unfavorable for the blossoming of socialist democracy. Like the proletariat, it is fundamentally attached to collective ownership of the means of production and opposed to capitalism: that is why Stalin finally crushed the kulaks and stood up against the Nazi invasion. It has not destroyed the basic socioeconomic conquests of the October Revolution; on the contrary, it has conserved them, be it by means that enter more and more into conflict with the basic goals of socialism. The socialized mode of production born of the October Revolution has withstood successfully all assaults from outside and all undermining from within. It has proved its superiority to hundreds of millions of human beings. This is the basic historical trend which, incidentally, also explains why world revolution, instead of being definitively thrown back for decades as pessimists assumed, could so easily rise again and conquer momentous victories after World War II.

But unlike the proletariat, it is basically conservative in outlook, afraid of any new upsurge of world revolution, because it feels that this would trigger a new stage of workers' militancy inside its own country, which would threaten its own power and privileges. The theory and practice of "socialism in one country" in the twenties and thirties, like the theory and practice of "peaceful coexistence" in the fifties and sixties, are a perfect expression of the socially contradictory nature of that bureaucracy. It will certainly defend itself when threatened with extinction by imperialism; it will even try to extend its "zone of influence" when this can be done without upsetting the social equilibrium of forces on a world scale. But it is basically attached to the status quo. American statesmen have found this out, in the long run. Krassó should show at least their aware-

---

[4] As we know today, Stalin also tried to influence the Yugoslav and Chinese Communists against conquering power. He instructed the Vietnamese CP to stay inside the French colonial empire, rechristened the "French Union." The party he had educated obstinately refused to engage upon Fidel Castro's road toward a victorious socialist revolution in Cuba for several years. Don't these facts need a *sociological* and not a simply *psychological* explanation?

ness of this rationale of Russian foreign policy since Lenin's death, and he should try to find a social explanation for this consistent behavior. He will find no other than the one that Trotsky elaborated.

The bureaucracy and its apologists can, of course, try and rationalize that policy, stating that it was merely concerned with the defense of the Soviet Union against the threat of all capitalists ganging up against it, if "provoked" by revolutions elsewhere. In the same way social democrats have consistently argued that they oppose revolutions only in order to defend the working-class organizations and conquests, which would be crushed by reaction if the bourgeoisie was "provoked" by revolutionary activity. But Marx taught us precisely not to judge parties and social groups on the basis of their self-rationalizations and self-proclaimed intentions, but on the basis of their objective role in society and the objective results of their actions. In that sense, the true social nature of the Soviet bureaucracy is reflected in the sum total of its actions, in the same way that, according to Lenin, the true social nature of the trade-union bureaucracy and the petit-bourgeois top echelons of social democracy in the imperialist countries *explains* their consistent opposition to socialist revolution.

Here we are again at our starting point. Marxists understand the relative autonomy of political institutions, but this understanding implies a constant research into the social roots of these institutions and into the social interests that they serve in the last analysis. It also implies that the more these institutions rise above the social classes that they first were said to serve, the more they succumb, independently of their own will, to a tendency toward self-defense and self-perpetuation, and the more they can enter into conflict with the historical interests of the class from which they arose. This is the way Marx and Lenin understood the problem. In this sense, Krassó's charge that Trotsky "underestimated" the possibility of autonomy of "parties" and "nations" is just an accusation that he was a Marxist and a Leninist. We are sure that Trotsky would have been willing to carry the cross of that sin with stoicism and not without satisfaction.

15
Trotsky as Writer

Although exile in 1929 effectively ended the active and meaningful period of Trotsky's political life, it also permitted him much greater opportunity for writing. His early exile years resulted in the publication of his autobiography, My Life, *and the three-volume study,* History of the Bolshevik Revolution.

Bertram Wolfe, a veteran and somewhat hostile observer of the Soviet scene, examines Trotsky's literary talents and contribution to historical literature. His main focus is on The Russian Revolution.

BERTRAM WOLFE [1]

Like Thucydides, Xenophon and Josephus, Napoleon and Churchill, Leon Trotsky had to wait to write his major history until defeat had deprived him of the possibility of making history. But all his life he was a writer by avocation, and a history-maker by vocation. "Beginning in 1897," he wrote in his autobiography, "I have waged the fight chiefly with a pen in my hand." When he was writing for *Iskra* he chose a *nom de guerre*—not to say *nom de plume;* it was *Pero,* the Russian word for *pen.*

Unlike Lenin, Trotsky looked often at himself in the mirror of history and consciously treasured his personal historic role. After 1905, in which year he played a more important part than any other revolutionary leader, he chose the first moment of respite, exile in Vienna, to write *Die Russische Revolution: 1905* (Vienna, 1908 and 1909). It is a book of 334 oversized octavo pages of social analysis, history, political polemics, personal narrative, and apologia. At present forbidden in Russia, out of print in Germany,

[1] From Bertram D. Wolfe, *Strange Communists I Have Known* (London: George Allen and Unwin Ltd., 1966), pp. 196–206. Copyright © 1965 by Bertram D. Wolfe. Reprinted by permission of George Allen and Unwin Ltd., and Stein and Day/Publishers.

and never published in English, it remains an extremely important source for the study of the 1905 revolution.

Leon Trotsky did not find time to woo the muse of history again until 1929 found him once more in exile from his native land, for the third and last time, on the Turkish island of Prinkipo. Then he wrote two works of major importance to the historian: his autobiography (1929), which of necessity contains much history; and his *History of the Russian Revolution* (Vol. I, 1930, Vols. II and III, 1932), which contains much autobiography, although he always refers to himself in the third person.

The first thing to note about Trotsky as historian is that we are dealing with a persuasive and frequently pedantic polemicist who was both a great orator and a great master of literary style. He is proud of the year 1917, telling of it as an old soldier reliving his greatest battles, for in it his role was huge, and his whole life until 1917 was dedicated to bringing about the seizure of power "by the proletariat," with which the year ends. If Lenin provided the party machine and the conspirative bent and concentration on power, it was Trotsky who provided the central doctrine and the actual military-political strategy of the armed conquest of power. Trotsky's skillful and eloquent pen is here dedicated to the glorification of the Bolshevik seizure of power, the defense of his own role in it, and to the scorn, mockery, caricature, gross and cruel misrepresentation of all the defeated—a scorn that is more cruel when he deals with liberals, democrats, and the other socialist factions or parties than when he deals with the Tsar, the monarchists, or the reactionaries.

Decorativeness, metaphor, and verbal fireworks come naturally to Trotsky. Thus of Skobelev, formerly his follower and in 1917 a leader of the Executive Committee of the Soviet, he writes: "He conveyed the impression of a student playing the role of statesman on a home-made stage." Of Chernov: "Abstention from voting became for him a form of political life." Of Kerensky: "His strength in the period of dual power lay in his combining the weaknesses of liberalism with the weaknesses of democracy." Of the Tsar: "Nicholas inherited from his ancestors not only a giant empire, but also a revolution. And they did not bequeath him one quality which would have made him capable of governing an empire . . . Or even a county." Of the mob: "A revolution is always distinguished by impoliteness, probably because the ruling classes did not take the trouble in good season to teach the people fine manners." Of the Chairman of the Duma: "Rodzyanko tried to put down the revolution with the aid of a fire hose: he wept." Of the Provisional Government: "It sneaked on tiptoe around the blaze of the revolution, choking from the smoke, and saying to itself: let it burn down to the embers, then we'll try to cook up something." Of the socialists in the first coalition government: "Being obliged to enter the government in the name of the interests of the Entente front . . . the Socialists took upon themselves a third of the power, and the whole of the war." Bernard Shaw, himself no mean wielder of the snicker-snee, wrote of this history: "When Trotsky cuts off his opponent's head, he holds it up to show that there are no brains in it."

As an orator in 1917, and still as an historian in the 1930's Trotsky's first aim was to inflame the passions of the multitude, above all the passion of hatred. Not so much hatred of the Old Regime, which he detested coldly, pedantically, almost dispassionately, and which in any case was already dead and a mere ghost six weeks before Lenin returned to try to overthrow "the freest government in the world," and ten weeks before Trotsky reached Russia. Rather, it was to inflame hatred of liberals, democrats, liberal socialists, democratic socialists, pacifists, defenders of the new Russia and of that government which, unlike the one Lenin and Trotsky would set up, had the grace to regard itself as merely pre-legitimate and to call itself "provisional."

As an orator Trotsky was most effective at those moments in history when the normally passive and inchoate mass of unorganized men and women were stirred and shaken out of their habitual responses, and bewildered and made desperate by the mounting chaos of war, breakdown, and revolution. Then Leon Trotsky was able to move the mass chorus to the center of the stage, give it a sense of its own importance, enormous though transitory (in Trotsky's intentions and still more in Lenin's, the independent activity of the masses was meant to be transitory); then he could turn bewilderment and frustration into credulity concerning easy solutions and into anger, hatred, distrust, and scorn for all and sundry, except the Bolsheviks.

One of Trotsky's favorite audiences and participants in the mass scenes he staged were the sailors of Kronstadt. Having been held down by the despotic procedures of that tiny floating despotism, a battleship, they rose up against all commands, all discipline, all government. They rejected not only the Provisional Government but the All-Russian Soviet as well, setting up their "independent Soviet Republic." They jailed their officers without trial in the same hell holes that had been used to discipline them, and drowned or bloodily lynched many. "The most hateful," Trotsky observes, "were shoved under the ice," of course while still alive. "Bloody acts of retribution," he adds sententiously, "where as inevitable as the recoil of a gun." Even when, for once, Trotsky tried to restrain the hatred he was playing upon (they were about to lynch Chernov), he did not forget to employ flattery: "You have come here, you red men of Kronstadt, as soon as you heard of the danger threatening the revolution." When he stood on Anchor Square in Kronstadt, egging on the sailors against the Provisional Government and the Executive Committee of the Soviet, he said: "I tell you heads must roll, blood must flow. . . . The strength of the French Revolution was in the machine that made the enemies of the people shorter by a head. This is a fine device. We must have it in every city."

In 1921, Trotsky would direct picked troops headed by delegates to a Bolshevik Congress across the ice to reduce the "flower of the revolution" to submission, because they did not know when to stop self-activity and anarchic opposition to dictatorial rule, but this episode falls outside the scope of Trotsky's three volumes.

As a "Marxist" historian, Trotsky begins his work with an economic picture, proceeding from that to class structure, class struggles, class parties, and a class analysis of each action, speech, proposal, personage.

The economic picture begins with an account of Russia's backwardness, which to Trotsky has enormous advantages. These are not the ones usually noted, namely, that the later a country enters into industrialism the more it finds to borrow from the latest techniques of other lands without having to pass through the earlier stages and without being saddled with many obsolete and obsolescent plants. The advantages as Trotsky sees them are mainly political, and give rise to his enunciation of what he regards as the "fundamental law" of the Russian Revolution.

First, the more backward the economy, the weaker will be the bourgeoisie and the more retarded the democratic structure, which Trotsky ties dogmatically to what he calls the "bourgeois democratic revolution." Hence when Russia borrows the techniques of modern heavy industry, it creates a proletariat that is more concentrated, more powerful, and of course, more revolutionary than the bourgeoisie. Hence Trotsky's slogan of "No tsar but a workers' government." The bourgeoisie is expendable, and along with it, the "democratic revolution" identified by him with its rule.

Second, the later in history a revolution occurs, the more "advanced" and "modern" is the ideology which it can import. Russia is overthrowing tsarism in the twentieth century, which—again dogmatically—is one century too late for a democratic revolution or a constituent assembly. "In the middle of the seventeenth century," Trotsky writes, "the bourgeois revolution in England developed under the guise of a religious reformation." In the eighteenth century, France was able to skip the Reformation. In the twentieth, after the flourishing of Marxist socialism, "just as France stepped over the Reformation, so Russia stepped over the formal democracy."

The Soviet dictatorship is, by definition, the dictatorship of the proletariat. (Writing in 1930–32 Trotsky gives no sign that it has turned out to be the dictatorship of the party over all classes, including the workingmen, in the proletariat's name.) Hence it dispenses with "pure democracy" as the French Revolution did with "the Reformation." These propositions concerning "backwardness" and "borrowing" form the core of Trotsky's famous "law of combined development."

This "general law" leads to innumerable deductions, inferences, corollaries, and *obiter dicta*, of which the following is a typical example:

> We may lay this down as a law: Revolutionary governments are the more liberal, the more tolerant, the more "magnanimous" to the reaction, the shallower their program, the more they are bound up with the past, the more conservative their role. And the converse: the more gigantic their tasks and the greater the number of vested rights and interests they are to destroy, the more concentrated will be the revolutionary power, the more naked its dictatorship.

Such propositions are invariably treated as self-evident, and are at hand to settle any question.

No less self-evident, and easy to manipulate dogmatically, does our historian find the concept of class. For Trotsky it is an axiom that only one class must lead in a twentieth-century revolution, and only one emerge from it as the sole and necessarily dictatorial ruler: namely, the proletariat. It is no less axiomatic that there is only one party that is proletarian and socialist; all the rest are bourgeois, or —at once more gently and more scornfully—petty bourgeois.

If a party believes that the people (narod) should make the revolution and the people should rule, and that narod includes both peasants and workers, and even intellectuals—as did the Socialist Revolutionary Party—that party is petty bourgeois. Even if a party shares the same program with the Bolsheviks, as the Mensheviks did between 1903 and 1919, that does not entitle it to the cachet of proletarian or socialist. Those are accolades reserved by history for the Bolsheviks, the party of Lenin and Trotsky. This makes all political history beautifully simple.

Any resolution of the Soviet Executive, made up overwhelmingly until October 1917 of Socialist Revolutionaries and Mensheviks, with a Bolshevik minority, is automatically a bourgeois decision, unless the Bolsheviks propose and vote for it.

The Moscow City Duma, elected by a vote that was 58 per cent Socialist Revolutionary, a little under 12 per cent Menshevik, and a few percentage points less Bolshevik, with about 17 per cent Constitutional Democrats and virtually no reactionaries, whenever it takes a decision against the vote of the Bolsheviks, is said to represent the bourgeoisie or the "pressure of bourgeois circles."

The war is equally uncomplicated. It is bourgeois imperialist by definition. Hence all who wish to continue it—even if they overthrow Miliukov for giving expression to "imperialist aims," if they try to force on the Allies and the Central Powers an early peace without victors or vanquished, if they are for self-determination for all peoples, even if they are merely in favor of defending revolutionary Russia against invasion, or for an early separate peace without further revolution in Russia and without world revolution—they are all bourgeois imperialist by definition.

The problems of power—of provisional government, dual power, soviet power, constituent assembly, democracy, and dictatorship—are solved just as easily and infallibly by the chanted formulae of this sorcerer's apprentice. The Provisional Government is capitalist by definition. The dual power is a simultaneous rule by "two classes," the one "the bourgeoisie" grouped around the Provisional Government, and the other, that of "the workers and soldiers," grouped around the Soviet. That makes the Provisional Government, *ipso facto,* bourgeois. But if the Soviet does not take all power into its hands, and continues to support the Provisional Government, that makes the Soviet majority, its leadership, and its actions, bourgeois too. Or petty bourgeois. (The petty bourgeois seems to be one who is bourgeois by definition, without knowing it.)

What if the Soviet should take all power, the slogan around which the epic battle is waged throughout most of these three volumes? One would think that this must represent the triumph of the proletariat. But not so fast! The Soviets, from February through September, still have a democratic socialist, hence a petty bourgeois, majority. The seizure of all power by the Soviet would only transfer the battle for power to a more favorable battleground. Only when the Bolsheviks have won a majority will this organization of "workers and soldiers" become "proletarian." And then its proletarian transfiguration will be automatic. "Only the guiding layers" (he means thereby the Bolshevik Party) "have a political program. . . . Without a guiding organization the energy of the masses would dissipate like steam which is not enclosed in a piston-box."

Clearly the Constituent Assembly is no proper piston box or piston for the steam of the locomotive of history. This, too, is clear by definition, for the Constituent Assembly is nineteenth century; it represents "pure" or "formal" democracy; it gives representation to the nation, the whole people, that is, all classes of the population. Hence it cannot serve twentieth-century socialism nor the proletarian dictatorship nor the rule of the "guiding layers." Any who in 1917 work for the fulfillment of the century-old dream that the Russian people should at long last determine their own destiny in freedom and write for themselves a charter of public liberties and social reforms, are fit only to be condemned as at best petty bourgeois, to be cast aside, and, in the end, denied the freedom to form a party or voice a program. Those who urge that land committees prepare a fair and systematic transfer of the land to the peasants, but want to wait for the completion of the program and its ratification by the Constituent Assembly, are caught in the same net of annihilation by labels.

It is true that on the eve of the seizure of power, when Trotsky delivered his presidential address on his election to the presidency of the Petrograd Soviet, he solemnly pledged: "We shall conduct the work of the Petrograd Soviet in a spirit of lawfulness and of full freedom for all parties. The hand of the Presidium will never lend itself to the suppression of the minority."

But as historian, Trotsky prefers to forget this pledge. This is one time he neglects to record the unforgettable words of Leon Trotsky. When Sukhanov, three years after the Bolshevik seizure of power, reminded him of the pledge, he lapsed into silence for a while, then said wistfully: "Those were good days."

I cannot close this all too brief analysis of these three stout volumes without at least a word on what the historian will find in them.

First, there is a powerful and eloquent statement of the doctrines and dogmas that guided Lenin and Trotsky in 1917.

Second, there are brilliant word pictures of scenes of revolution and masses in action.

Third, there are remarkable profiles, one-sided and unfair to the point of caricature, but always vivid and revealing, of all the principle actors.

Fourth, there is an account, unparalleled in historical literature, of the strategy and tactics, the military moves, in the preparation of the deceptive conspiracy of October to seize power under the guise of merely defending the revolution. Trotsky exults in his skill in disguising every step in the offensive as a defensive action, and enjoys now his recollection and meticulous exposition after the events of all the details which he knew better than any other man, even Lenin; for it was he, as Chairman of the Military Revolutionary Committee and Petrograd Soviet, who plotted every step, wrapped each maneuver in the brazen impudence of his eloquence, and personally directed the fulfillment of each measure. The chapters on the "Military Revolutionary Committee" and on the "Conquest of the Capital" are not equaled by all the other literature on the event put together.

Fifth, this history lays bare, both where it intends and where it does not intend, the soul of one of the principal actors in the October seizure of power—at the brief moment of consummation, the most important actor.

Finally, it is a history which no historian of Russia and no historian of revolution can afford to neglect. But let him be forewarned that Trotsky's is a pen that is frequently as persuasive as it is continuously one-sided. It is always the historian's duty, too often neglected out of worship of the bitch-goddess Success, to seek out the truths of the defeated along with the truths that get published by the victors. But particularly here must the reader come well equipped with an awareness of the truths of the defeated—the more so because somewhere concealed in this blinding flood of words which record the victory of Trotsky and his party, are also some of the secrets which explain why Trotsky, too, must in the end be reckoned as one of the defeated.

Bibliographical Note

The literature on Trotsky is not as plentiful as one would expect, and what does exist is of a very uneven quality. The best general accounts of his place in revolutionary history are to be found in the various volumes of E. H. Carr, *History of the Bolshevik Revolution* (London, 1950–60), and Robert V. Daniels, *The Conscience of the Revolution* (Cambridge, Mass., 1960).

Trotsky's autobiography, *My Life* (New York, 1970), is a surprisingly objective account and is a good source to begin with. Two biographies covering his early years are G. Ziv, *Trotsky. Kharakteristika po Lichnym Vospominaniam* (New York, 1921), not available in English translation, and Max Eastman, *Leon Trotsky: Portrait of a Youth* (New York, 1925). A very flattering account of Trotsky's career is provided by Victor Serge, *Vie et Mort de Trotsky* (Paris, 1951). The major biography to date is the monumental three-volume study by Isaac Deutscher, *The Prophet Armed, Trotsky: 1879–1921* (London, 1954); *The Prophet Unarmed, Trotsky: 1921–1929* (London, 1959); *The Prophet Outcast, Trotsky: 1929–1940* (London, 1963). A forthcoming biography by Joel Carmichael will be published shortly by Hodder and Stoughton. A preview of Carmichael's book is presented in two of his essays, "The Agony of a Revolutionary," *Encounter* XXXVIII, no. 5 (May, 1972), 31–41; XXXVIII, no. 6 (June, 1972), 28–36. An interesting attempt at psychoanalysis is presented in E. Victor Wolfenstein, *The Revolutionary Personality: Lenin, Trotsky, and Ghandi* (Princeton, 1967). A recent book by Joseph Nedava, *Trotsky and the Jews* (Philadelphia, 1972), throws considerable light on the subject.

Three literary attempts to portray the problems of Trotsky's life are: Bernard Wolfe, *The Great Prince Died* (New York, 1959), a novel of dubious merit; Berthold Brecht's exciting play *Galileo Galilei* (London, 1960); and a more recent play by Peter Weiss, *Trotsky in Exile* (London, 1971).

Intimate character sketches of Trotsky by individuals who knew him personally are to be found in the following: B. Bajanov, *Avec Staline dans le Kremlin* (Paris, 1930); A. Balabanoff, *My Life as a Rebel* (London, 1938); Louis Fischer, *Men and Politics* (New York, 1946); L. Frossard, *De Jaurès à Lénine* (Paris, 1930); A. Morizet, *Chez Lénine et Trotski* (Paris, 1922); A. Rosmer *Moscou sous Lénine* (Paris, 1953).

Books dealing with the assassination are: A. Goldman, *The Assassination of Leon Trotsky* (New York, no date), and I. Don Levine, *The Mind of an Assassin* (New York, 1959).

There is a growing body of articles and periodical literature on various aspects of Trotsky's life. His internment in Canada before returning to Russia is treated in W. Rodney, "Broken Journey: Trotsky in Canada 1917," *Queen's Quarterly*, 1967, 74(4): 649–665.

References to Trotsky's military role are found in: David Footman, "The Red Army and the Civil War in the East," *History Today*, 1955 6(2): 96–102; Malcolm Macintosh, "The Development of Soviet Military Doctrine Since 1918," in *Theory and Practice of War: Essays Presented to Captain B. H. Liddell Hart on His Seventieth Birthday* (New York, 1966), and R. Schlesinger, "Trotsky in the Crises of the Civil War," *Science and Society*, 1966, 31(1): 48–58. Simon Liberman, *Building Lenin's Russia* (Chicago, 1945), provides a brief description of Trotsky's celebrated armored train.

Trotsky's participation in the crushing of the Kronstadt rebellion is discussed in G. Scheuer, "Kronstadt, März 1921," *Zukunft*, 1957 (3): 84–86 and Franz Zölch, "Kronstadt Vor Viezig Jahren," *Schweizer Monatshefte*, 1961, 40(12): 1183–1186.

Articles dealing with theoretical aspects of Trotsky's works are: G. Procacci, "Trotsky's View of the Critical Years, 1929–1936," *Science and Society*, 1963, 27(1): 62–69; H. Brahm, "La 'Revolution Permanente' De Trotski et le 'Socialisme Dans un Seul Pays' de Staline," *Cahiers du Monde Russe et Sovietique*, 1965 6(1): 84–99; N. Valentinov, "De la 'NEP' a la Collectivisation," *Contrat Social*, 1964 8(2): 72–82; H. Schurer, "The Permanent Revolution," *Survey*, 1960 (32): 68–73.

A recent and disappointing Soviet publication, *Against Trotskyism* (Moscow, 1972), is a tedious compilation of almost every negative statement on the subject since 1903.

Trotsky's manuscript material was sold to Harvard University and is deposited in the Houghton Library. Several sections of the archive are sealed and will remain so until 1980. The most useful bibliography of Trotsky's writings is Louis Sinclair, *Leon Trotsky: A Bibliography* (California, 1972).

Index

Due **28** Days From Latest Date

OCT 3 1973			
DEC 5 1973			
JAN 1 2 1974			
MAR 1 1 1974			
MAY 1 1 1974			
NOV 1 4 1990		WITHDRAWN